The Catholic Companion to Mary

God bless you. Mary keep you!
Sr. Mary Kathleen Glavich, SND.

Mary Kathleen Glavich, SND

PUBLICATIONS

The Catholic Companion to Mary
by Mary Kathleen Glavich, SND

Edited by Gregory F. Augustine Pierce
Cover design by Tom A. Wright
Cover art by M.P. Wiggens, www.thespiritsource.com
Interior art by Dan Paulos and Mary Jean Dorcy, OP
Text Design and Typesetting by Desktop Edit Shop, Inc.

Scripture quotations are from the *New Revised Standard Version Bible,* copyright © 1989 by the Division of Christian Education of the National Council of the Churches of Christ in the USA. Used by permission.

"The Litany of Mary of Nazareth" on pages 170-172 is reprinted with permission from Pax Christi USA, 532 West Eighth Street, Erie, PA 16502. For more information on Pax Christi USA, the national Catholic peace movement, visit www.paxcrhistiusa.org.

Copyright © 2007 by Mary Kathleen Glavich, SND

Published by ACTA Publications, 5559 W. Howard Street, Skokie, IL 60077-2621, (800) 397-2282, www.actapublications.com

Library of Congress Catalog number: 2007926217

ISBN-10: 0-87946-330-9
ISBN-13: 978-0-87946-330-4
Printed in the United States of America

Year 12 11 10 09 08 07
Printing 8 7 6 5 4 3 2 1

The Catholic Companion to Mary

Dedicated with love to
Sister Mary Sujita Kallupurakkathu, SND,
who reflects Mary's qualities
and truly acts as her sister in the world.

Introduction

She asked him, "What should I call you?
Man? But your conception is divine.
God? But you are clothed with our flesh and blood.
What shall I do for you? Shall I nurse you with my milk or glorify you?
Shall I care for you like a mother or worship you like a maidservant?
Shall I kiss you like my son or pray to you like my God?
Should I give you milk or incense?
What an ineffable mystery!
Heaven uses you as a throne and you lie in my arms!
You give yourself wholly to the inhabitants of the earth,
Yet you do not deprive heaven of your presence."

St. Basil

In Amy Tan's novel, *The Joy Luck Club,* four young women who are estranged from their mothers to varying degrees come to understand them after hearing the stories of their lives back in China. This new knowledge lets each girl truly see her mother for the first time and leads to a deeper relationship between mother and daughter.

Mary, the mother of Jesus, was given to us by him as a gift when he was hanging on the cross, looking down on her and the "beloved disciple" (who stood for all of us). Jesus told the disciple: "Behold your mother." This heavenly mother of ours is even more of a mystery to us than Tan's Chinese mothers were to their daughters. Twenty centuries stretch between her life on earth and ours. Because Mary's culture didn't approve of making images, we have no contemporary paintings or statues of her. She didn't leave anything in writing, and what was written about her is sparse—a few passages in the Gospels.

Since Mary's life is wrapped in mystery, no one can write a real biography of her. Our concept of Mary has been shaped by the Scripture, Church teachings, legends, pious traditions, apparitions such as those at Lourdes and Fatima, and religious art—everything from Byzantine icons to contemporary Christmas cards.

Mary is our mother not only because Jesus said so but because by cooperating with God she gave us new life by bringing her son, the Savior, into the world. Where Eve is the mother of all the living, Mary, a daughter of Eve, is our mother on the spiritual plane. When the human race was spiritually dead because of sin and could no longer look forward to eternal life, we were reborn as new creatures by the sacrifice of Jesus and can now share God's life again and hope to possess eternal life. Mary's mission in the divine plan of salvation is therefore unique.

Catholics have been criticized for treating Mary like God or for speaking about and to Mary in terms that should be reserved for God alone. It is certainly true that before the Second Vatican Council and recent development of the theology of the Holy Spirit, there was a period in history when Catholics in their exuberance for Mary did ascribe to her divine powers and attributes that she just cannot have. In some people's minds, Mary the mother became equated with God the Father. True Catholic devotion to Mary, however, distinguishes between adoration owed God and honor given to Mary. It recognizes that Mary is one of us, a created human being. In that way, she is our sister as well as our mother.

Moreover, we know that everything that is good and beautiful in Mary is from God. Mary is like the moon, which shines only because it reflects the light from the sun. As many spiritual writers have pointed out, Mary shines brightest at night, when we are most in darkness. And Mary can't be separated from her son Jesus. Her maternal relationship to him made her what she is today. Therefore any honor given to Mary is essentially *Christocentric*, that is, Christ-centered.

Attitudes toward Mary vary, even among Catholics. Some people, due to the misguided thinking of certain past cultures, regard her almost as a goddess—lofty and superhuman. To them her perfection and purity make her unapproachable and as cold as some of the stiff statues that represent her. On the other hand, many people—Catholic and non-Catholic alike—think of Mary as someone near and dear to them in a real and very personal way.

So who is the real Mary, and what role does she play in our lives? *The Catholic Companion to Mary* is an attempt to bring Mary to life as a flesh-and-blood person, using what research and theological study and the experience of millions of Catholics have revealed about her. Just as restoring old paintings involves removing the encrustations, damages and touch-ups of the centuries, today's Church works to peel away the accumulations that obscure the true, original Mary. We find that although Mary lived in a culture totally different from ours and was a one-of-a-kind human being, we can still discover characteristics from her life that give meaning to our own.

This book presents what the Catholic Church believes about Mary and a wealth of intriguing information about people's devotion to her. While knowing about the Mother of God is important, this book's paramount purpose is not merely to impart knowledge. Rather, these pages are meant to act as a telescope that brings Mary more into focus, so that the reader may be drawn into a stronger relationship with her and ultimately with God.

Holy Mary
God's Chosen One

Of all the billions of women who have existed or will exist, Mary is the one God chose to play a special role in salvation—to be his mother, enabling him to become human in order to save us from sin and death. That is why the Church in one of its earliest official pronouncements called her the "Mother of God." What do we know about this unique woman? Very little, really. The scant knowledge we have of her is gleaned from Scripture, and now some scholars are speculating that the Scripture stories about her are more symbolic than historical. We do know, though, that Mary was a real woman—a woman who experienced poverty, oppression, exile, violence, and the unjust execution of her son. Yet she was a woman in whom God obviously delighted.

The first line of a Flemish hymn is "Love gave her a thousand names." For twenty centuries Christians have cherished Mary, giving her titles that reflect their love and admiration such as Queen, Our Lady, Daystar, and Mystical Rose. In the beginning though, Mary was simply Mary (or in her language Miriam or Miryam) of Nazareth. Miriam was also the name of Moses' sister, who helped lead the Israelites out of bondage in Egypt to the promised land. In Hebrew literature, Miryam is said to mean "bitter." Other interpretations are "the beloved of Yahweh" or "the beautiful one." Recent archeological finds suggest that Mary means "sublime one."

Among the Hebrews the name Mary was so popular that in the Gospels we find what writer Marina Warner called "a muddle of Marys." Today, because of Mary of Nazareth, more women and girls in the United States have the name Mary than any other name. In some countries it's been the custom to give boys the name Mary or Marie as well, usually as a second name.

*There's never enough
said or written about
Mary.*

—St. Anselm

Worship of God is
called *adoration* or
latria. Honor given
to the saints is
veneration or *dulia*,
and veneration of
Mary is *hyperdulia*.

Mary is now world-renowned. She has been the subject of more art, literature and music than any other woman. At least eight times, she's been on the cover of *Time* magazine, and U.S. postage stamps picturing her and her son are issued every year for Christmas. Yet Mary belonged to the working class and was not famous or wealthy. She was as obscure and inconsequential as other women of her day. As far as we know, she worked no miracles, never preached or baptized, wrote no books or pamphlets, and her special graces and privileges were hidden from public view.

In the whole New Testament, Mary is mentioned only nineteen times. St. Paul's letters, which were written before the Gospels, never refer to Mary by name. We find only these words: "But when the fullness of time had come, God sent his Son, born of a woman, born under the law, in order to redeem those who were under the law, so that we might receive adoption as children" (Galatians 4:4–5). Neither does the *Didache*, the Church's oldest teaching document, mention Mary. In fact, it took centuries after this woman lived on earth for the Church to recognize and formulate everything we believe about her today. Each era brings new insights into and new attitudes toward the mystery that is Mary. Our age is no different.

Physical Attributes

Mary must have been strong and robust with roughened hands, considering the daily tasks of Jewish women as well as the strenuous journeys the Gospels say she undertook. She most likely had the long dark hair, tan skin, and dark eyes characteristic of Middle Eastern women. Then again, if King David, who had auburn hair, was her ancestor, perhaps she took after him. Visionaries who claim to have seen Mary in apparitions say that her eyes are deep blue. When St. Bernadette of Lourdes was shown images of Mary and asked which looked most like her, the saint replied that none of them came close to capturing the beauty of the original lady she had seen.

The artists of different nations often depict Mary and her son as one of their own people. In Korea, Mary and Jesus look Asian, in Africa they look Black, and in the United States they can appear as blue-eyed blonds. This chameleon-like characteristic illustrates the universality of Mary and Jesus. All peoples identify with them and claim them as their own. In fact, when a class of fourth-graders drew pictures of Mary, one girl showed her wearing their school uniform!

a cool website...

Take a virtual tour of the Holy land by going to www.ffhl.org/virtualtourhl.asp.

Mary's Parents

When biographical information about Mary was lacking, imagination and devotion to her created it. A number of apocryphal (unofficial) gospels were written in the first centuries of the Church. Although these sometimes contain preposterous stories, some may enshrine nuggets of truth transmitted by oral tradition.

The apocryphal *Protoevangelium of James* (also called *The Nativity of Mary),* which was written about 150 A.D., tells us that Mary was born to a Jewish couple named Joachim and Anne. According to this document, Anne was barren and, consequently, wealthy Joachim's alms weren't accepted in the Temple. Joachim went for a forty-day fast in the desert to persuade God to help. There an angel revealed to him that his wife Anne was pregnant and sent Joachim to her. An angel had also announced to Anne that she would have a child. Anne and Joachim met at the Golden Gate in

In the musical *West Side Story,* the hero sings a song in praise of the name Maria. A number of other popular girls' names in various countries are forms of Mary: Maretta, Mariah, Marie, Mariel, Marian, Marion, Marianne, Mariella, Marieta, Marietta, Maresa, Marika, Marja, Marija, Marua, Maureen, Marilyn, Mae, Manette, Marice, Muire and Rosemary. Nicknames based on Mary are Mai, Maia, Maja, Mame, Mamie, Manon, Masha, May, Maya, Mia, Mimi, Mitzi, Mollie, Molly, Polly and Ria. Other girls' names are based on devotion to Mary: Annunciata, Assumpta, Dolores, Virginia, Immaculata, Lourdes, Guadalupe, Lupe, Pilar, and Rosaria.

Jerusalem and embraced. The Church celebrates a feast day for these grandparents of Jesus on July 26.

St. Anne, who had the distinct privilege of bringing up Mary, is the patron of grandmothers, housewives, and pregnant women. One of the most popular sites in the Holy Land is the Basilica of St. Anne near the Temple, presumably built over the childhood home of Mary. Another shrine in her honor is the Basilica of St. Anne de Beaupré in Quebec, Canada. Built in 1658, it was the first pilgrimage shrine in North America.

The Immaculate Conception

Many people mistakenly believe that the doctrine of the Immaculate Conception refers to the way Jesus was conceived. Instead, it refers to *Mary* herself. Catholics believe that in some mysterious way Mary must have been preserved from original sin from the first moment of her existence. This teaching is not found directly in the Scriptures but rather developed over the centuries in popular Catholic belief. It was based on the idea that in light of Mary's unique role as the Mother of God she would have had to be free of all sin, even the original sin that is shared by all human beings. In 1854, this belief was declared a dogma (a definite teaching) of the Catholic Church, called the *Immaculate Conception.*

Original sin is the fallen state of human nature that we're all born into, having inherited the separation from God caused by our first parents. Once the concept of original sin was developed by St. Augustine (354–430 A.D.), theologians began to consider Mary's relationship to it. They determined that Mary, as God's mother, was redeemed and received God's grace from the very moment of her conception by her parents, in anticipation of her unique role in salvation history. In other words, not for a moment was Mary in the snare of sin. Her exemption from original sin means that she always lived the destiny of the whole Church. As someone once put it: "God first created a man, Adam, but God began the new creation with a woman, Mary."

It makes sense that God would bestow this privilege on Mary and on her alone. First of all, it's only fitting that God, who is infinitely holy, should have a pure, spotless vessel bring him forth on earth. As Father Tom Fanta used to explain to children, "Jesus is God's best gift to us. When you wrap a present, you use beautiful wrapping paper and lovely ribbon. God wrapped his Son in the beautiful Virgin Mary." Second, God preserved Mary from sin because, after all, it was her son who conquered sin. Why should anyone object then that Jesus would make Mary the first fruit of his saving work and let her experience early what awaits the rest of us human beings? It helps to understand this mystery of Mary's pre-redemption when you consider that with God there is no time—everything is now. Third, Mary's freedom from original sin was an expression of God's love for her, his most beautiful creation, his masterpiece, his most highly favored daughter.

In addition to her being free from original sin, which left humanity with a tendency toward evil, Mary never committed a personal sin. This doesn't mean she had no temptations, made no mistakes, or felt no negative emotions like worry, discouragement, fear or anger. She did. Like us, Mary had to cooperate with God's grace; her holiness unfolded until she was all-holy. Although we don't usually call her Saint Mary, actually she is Queen of All Saints, closer to God than any other human being.

A title of Mary that acknowledges her goodness is Immaculate Heart of Mary. This parallels the title

a cool website...

The Marian Library/ International Marian Research Institute is located at the University of Dayton in Dayton, Ohio. This library holds the world's largest collection of printed materials on Mary. Its goal is to gather and present information about the Virgin Mary and to lead people to a loving knowledge of her. See www.udayton.edu/mary.

trivial tidbit...

The Mississippi River was originally named Conception by Fr. Jacques Marquette, S.J., who had a deep devotion to the Immaculate Conception. He explored the river with Louis Joliet in 1673.

Sacred Heart of Jesus, which we give her son. The heart, the symbol of love, is regarded as the center of one's being. By saying that Mary's heart is immaculate, we mean that Mary herself is spotless and pure, full of love. She is, in the words of the Protestant poet William Wordsworth, "our tainted nature's solitary boast."

So, while it may be difficult to understand or even to believe, the Immaculate Conception is a cool thing. We are all made in God's image and reflect something of God. Mary, however, was "full of grace" from the very beginning, which means she was full of God's life and totally united to God. So, in a way, looking at this woman and the way she lived, we can observe the feminine face of God.

Infancy and Childhood

The official Gospels don't give a clue about Mary's childhood. On the other hand, apocryphal gospels tell fantastic stories about her infancy. For example, the *Protoevangelium of James* relates that when Anne and Joachim brought three-year-old Mary to live in the Temple she danced for joy on the stairs and everyone loved her. There she lived like a little nun, was fed by angels, and carried out the task of sewing the Temple veil with scarlet and purple thread. Having Mary grow up in the Temple was a way to show that Mary fully belonged to God. In all probability, Mary grew up at home like any other Jewish girl in Galilee and had the basic human needs, feelings, fears and temptations that we all experience.

Mary certainly spoke Aramaic—a sister language of Hebrew—probably with a Galilean accent that was considered backwards by the more sophisticated people in southern Palestine. She also most likely heard Greek, Latin and Hebrew spoken in her

14

The United States and the Immaculate Conception

The first settlement and capital in the colony of Maryland (named after Queen Henrietta Maria of England) was called St. Mary's City. In 1792, John Carroll, the bishop of Baltimore, Maryland, and the first bishop in the United States, placed the new country under the protection of Mary under the title of the Immaculate Conception. Later, in 1847, Pope Pius IX officially proclaimed the Immaculate Conception the patroness of the United States. Today in her honor a magnificent basilica, the National Shrine of the Immaculate Conception, stands in Washington, D.C.

In 1920, there was a blessing for the building of this church. The Eucharist for that occasion was celebrated on the altar used by Bishop John Carroll. In 1959, the basilica opened, the largest church in the western hemisphere. Its upper church can accommodate six thousand. People continue to flock to the shrine and pray at its more than 65 chapels and oratories, many of them in honor of the particular Marian devotions of other countries from where immigrants have come to the United States. A recent addition is the Chapel of Our Lady of Hope, dedicated in 1994. It is a gift of actor and comedian Bob Hope and his wife, Dolores, in memory of Mr. Hope's mother.

a cool website...

Visit the basilica of the National Shrine of the Immaculate Conception at www.nationalshrine.com and click on "Virtual Tour."

fyi...

New Advent, the Catholic Encyclopedia online, is dedicated to the Immaculate Heart of Mary.

town and probably knew a few words of each.

As a baby, Mary played with a rattle, and when she was a child she played outside with other children because it would have been dark in the house. Jews believed that making images was against the first commandment, which forbade idols, so Mary never had a doll or a puppet. She and her young friends and relatives played a form of hopscotch and made up their own games. Mary's family may have owned lambs, goats, or a donkey. If so, Mary would have helped care for them, taking them out to graze. Since cats abounded in Palestine, she might even have had one for a pet.

Some think that Mary had at least one sister, because John's Gospel states that Jesus' "mother's sister, Mary, the wife of Clopas" also stood at the foot of the cross. Since it's odd that two girls would be named Mary in the same family, this one could have been a sister-in-law, a relative of Joseph, or a cousin. No brothers are mentioned in the Bible, but Mary may have had a large extended family and some relatives may have lived with her and her parents.

Mary's Character

To people in her village, Mary was one of them, just Miriam, the daughter of Joachim and Anne. Catholics are sure, however, that Mary must have been an exceptionally good girl—obedient, helpful, responsible, kind and loving—because she would have possessed all the virtues, even at a young age. The word *virtue* comes from the Latin for "strength," and Mary proved through the actions of her life that she was not a passive wimp but a woman with backbone, one who deserves the title Tower of Strength that we give her in the Litany of Loreto.

Catholics believe Mary is a living portrait of the Beatitudes her son taught as a blueprint for Christian living: poor in spirit, mourning, meek, hungering and thirsting for righteousness, merciful, pure in heart, a peacemaker, and persecuted for righteousness' sake. Jesus exclaimed that the people he described in the Beatitudes are blessed. That Mary is blessed was confirmed by the Angel Gabriel and Elizabeth, who both addressed her as "blessed are you."

Mary and Abraham

Mary is often compared to Abraham, the first to believe in the one God, our ancestor in the faith. God had promised Abraham many descendants, but then asked him to sacrifice his son, Isaac. (Although, interestingly enough, most Muslims believe that it was his son Ishmael he tried to sacrifice.) After Abraham showed his willingness to obey, even though it would seem to block the possibility of any descendants, God spared his son and said to Abraham, "By your offspring shall all the nations of the earth gain blessing for themselves, because you have obeyed my voice" (Genesis 22:18). Through Mary's faith and obedience in the face of what was seemingly impossible and what she couldn't comprehend, the promise to her forefather Abraham was fulfilled. Her son was sacrificed to save all nations.

for your spiritual health...

Organize a group pilgrimage to the Shrine of the Immaculate Conception in Washington, D.C. Go to www.nationalshrine.com and click on "About the Shrine" and then "Schedule a Visit." If you cannot go now, have your group make a spiritual pilgrimage by saying all four sets of mysteries of the rosary together, including the Mysteries of Light, which were suggested by Pope John Paul II. (See pages 147-150 for a listing of all the mysteries.)

The word for "blessed" can also be translated as "happy." Mary must have been a cheerful person, someone others like to be around. To overcome all the difficulties of her life, she must have possessed the deep-down joy and calm that no one or no thing could dispel. Not only was Mary joyful herself, but by giving herself so freely to God's plan of salvation she brought joy to the world. And so another of her many titles is Cause of Our Joy.

Mary of Nazareth
First-Century Woman

ary was from the country of Palestine (today much of present-day Israel), which was about the size of the state of Vermont. Nazareth, where Mary lived most of her life, was an obscure little village in Palestine's hilly northern province of Galilee, about fifteen miles from the Sea of Galilee. Lists of Galilean cities at the time don't even include Nazareth, which shows how small it must have been. This town was held in such low esteem that when the apostle Nathaniel first met Jesus he wondered, "Can anything good come out of Nazareth?" (John 1:46). Jews from Judea, where the capital of Jerusalem was, scorned all of Galilee, calling it "Gentile Galilee" because of the many non-Jewish people who both lived in and passed through it.

Life in Nazareth

The farming village of Nazareth was home to not more than 500 people. They lived in white limestone houses along stony dirt roads. Some houses may have been grouped around a common courtyard. The homes were one room and had a lower level where animals were kept. The floor was packed-down dirt, but there could be a stone area, where the family ate and slept on the floor together on mats or rugs, wrapped in their garments. There were no nightgowns or pajamas in those days, nor much privacy for that matter!

Stairs outside led to the flat roof made of wooden beams and clay, where food could be dried and where it was cooler to sleep on hot summer nights. On the right doorpost of the house was a *mezuzah*, a small case containing

An International Mari-
an Center, comprised
of five large buildings,
is being constructed
opposite the Basilica
of the Annunciation in
Nazareth. This project,
initiated by the mayor
of Nazareth, involves
Catholic, Orthodox
and Protestant Chris-
tians. According to its
mission statement,
the Center will "allow
large crowds of peo-
ple the opportunity of
contemplating the
many aspects of
Mary's extraordinary
mystery and discover-
ing the depths of the
Christian faith." The
plan includes twelve
sister centers to be
built around the
world, including one
in Denver, Colorado.

a parchment with two Scripture quotations, one the *Shema*, the prayer that begins, "Hear, O Israel! The Lord is our God, the Lord alone!" (Deuteronomy 6:4) An opening in the *mezuzah* would reveal the title of God *"Shaddai,"* or just the "S." On leaving or entering the house, Mary would touch the opening with her fingers and then kiss them, similar to Catholics dipping their fingers in holy water fonts at doorways of churches or even their homes.

Inside the house were few furnishings—maybe a table and a few chairs or benches. Pottery was kept on ledges built into the walls. There were no windows or very small ones without glass. Light was provided by the open door and oil lamps, which were small bowls of olive oil with a wick hung over the side that gave the house a sweet, rancid odor.

Galilee had two seasons: a dry summer and a wet winter. The soil was fertile and watered from snow-capped Mount Hermon, which could be seen from the hills of Nazareth. The landscape was a pattern of wheat and barley fields and wildflowers, marked by cypress trees pointing to the sky like dark spears. Because there was no electricity or neon signs, the night sky was filled with hundreds of stars that looked close enough to touch. Galilee was a beautiful land that would invite Jesus, Mary and Joseph to lift their hearts and minds frequently to the Creator of heaven and earth.

Mary wore an ankle-length tunic, a wool one in the winter and a linen one in the summer. She is usually pictured in blue, and a favorite child's poem addresses her as "Lovely Lady, dressed in blue." It's possible that Mary's dress was indeed blue, the color of the sky and oceans. Indigo was a dye made from a plant that was plentiful in Palestine and is the only dye that can color flax, from which Mary's clothes would have been made. Moreover, we know that later on in history the everyday dresses of

Palestinian women were often blue.

If Mary wasn't barefoot, she wore sandals that were merely hide soles tied on with a cord. So her feet were always dusty. When she was older, Mary began to wear a veil on her head when she went outside. She might have had braided hair and probably wore glass or metal ornaments in it.

Boys were taught by their fathers from the age of three and then started going to synagogue school when they were six years old. Girls were not schooled at all. Therefore, Mary was illiterate. But since hers was an oral culture this wasn't as much of a handicap as it would be today. Instead of Hebrew, geography and history, Mary learned the domestic skills that would make her a good wife and mother.

It was probably Mary's job to fetch water from the one well in Nazareth. This well, called "Mary's Well" now, is still there. Pilgrims can dip a pail into its spring from inside a church. After chatting with the other girls and women at the well, Mary would balance the large clay water jar on her head, shoulder or hip and make her way home. She would also gather branches or dried grass as fuel for the fire. At harvest time, Mary worked in the fields, gathering the grain or the fruit.

Mary helped her mother prepare the two meals of the day—one in the morning and one in the evening. She learned the Jewish dietary laws, such as never to serve dairy products and meat at the same time. Because there was no refrigeration, food had to be bought every day at the market where Mary undoubtedly had to haggle for a good price, as was and still is the custom. Watching her mother, Mary would learn how to build a fire, care for and milk the animals, make cheese, and prepare bread by grinding the meal between two stones, mixing it with water, and baking it in a simple oven

I see you, Mary,
lovingly expressed
in a thousand pictures,
But none of them
can portray you,
as my soul
looks on you.

—Novalis

outside. She would help serve the food: usually wheat or barley bread, fish, cheese and fruit—mostly olives, pomegranates, grapes and figs. Seldom did the Jews of her time eat meat; and when they did, all the blood had to be drained from it. Instead of sugar, they used honey.

Seated with her family on the ground around a mat, Mary would eat with her fingers from a simple clay plate (there were no forks and spoons) and drink from a cup with no handle. For soups and stews, she would dip slices of bread into the common bowl. Afterwards she would help clear up and wash the dishes.

Mary's mother, Anne, taught her how to spin, weave cloth, and then sew wool and linen garments. Mary also helped wash clothes at a stream, pounding the dirt out of them with a rock and hanging them up to dry.

Mary's husband, Joseph, and their son, Jesus, lived with her, and she would do these services for them. Some of Jesus' analogies and parables (stories that teach a lesson) had their roots in homey scenes he remembered from living with her in Nazareth: yeast in dough, new wineskins, sweeping the floor for a lost coin, patching clothes.

Ordinary chores were Mary's daily routine all her life. As a simple housewife and mother, she carried out her main vocation to bring the light of Christ into the world. We all share this vocation, no matter what work we do. The Church teaches that all occupations are potential places for the "nativity" of Christ. All we need to do is echo Mary's "Let it be with me according to your word" (Luke 1:38).

A Hebrew Woman

In the patriarchal society of Mary's day, women were valued for their childbearing and their domes-

Our Lady of La Vang

In October of 2006, a new chapel in honor of Our Lady of La Vang opened in the Shrine of the Immaculate Conception in Washington. Catholicism has been in Vietnam since the early 1600s, and more than 130,000 have been martyred in persecutions. During one bitter persecution in 1798, some Catholics hid in the thick jungle of La Vang, where they suffered from the cold, wild animals, sickness, and hunger. At night they would gather in small groups to pray. One night the Blessed Virgin appeared to them wearing a long cape. She was surrounded by lights and held a child in her arms. Mary comforted the people and promised that their prayer there would be heard. She also told them to boil the leaves from the nearby trees as medicine for their illnesses. Mary appeared several more times at this place, near the 17th Parallel that divides North and South Vietnam. A shrine was erected there, which Pope John XXIII declared a basilica in 1962.

tic work, but they were expected to be neither seen nor heard. Most of the time they stayed at home. If a woman did venture out, she had to wear a veil. No man would speak in public to a woman who was not a relative.

Jewish women were subject first to their fathers, then their husbands. Even learning about the Torah (the Jewish law in the first five books of the Bible) was denied them. Women could not inherit anything as long as there was a man in the family. Their word was not accepted in court. And while wives could be divorced for something as simple as serving a bad meal, they could not divorce their husbands for any reason whatsoever.

Women were not even bound to follow the same religious practices as men, such as praying the

St. Bernardine of
Siena visualized
Mary's heart with
seven flames shooting
out from it to stand
for her acts of love
expressed in her
"seven words"–the
seven sayings of Mary
recorded in the
Gospels. See if you
can find all seven.

Shema three times a day or going to the Temple for
the three greatest Jewish feasts. When women did
visit the Temple, they were confined to the Court of
Women. In the local synagogues, the women did
not speak. No wonder that a daily Jewish man's
prayer was (and still is in some forms of Judaism):
"Thank you, God, that I was not born a woman."

Mary's son, Jesus, displayed a revolutionary atti-
tude toward women. Unlike the old covenant, in
which only men were initiated through circumci-
sion, the new covenant of Jesus offers initiation
through baptism for both men and women. He always treated women with respect and kindness.
Not only did Jesus repeatedly dare to speak to
women in public (for example, the Samaritan
woman, the Canaanite woman, the widow of
Nain), but when he did he spoke to them as an
equal, listening to them and valuing what they
said. When he rose from the dead, he chose to appear first to women, starting with Mary Magdalen,
not his male apostles. It was a woman, too, his
mother, who came to be known as Jesus' first and
best disciple. As Sojourner Truth declared, "The incarnation was between God and a woman. Men
had nothing to do with it." For good reason, the
Swiss pastor Kurt Marti called Mary's prime role in
salvation "her holy coup." She raised womanhood
to a new level.

Daughter of Abraham
Faithful Jewess

As a Jew, Mary is a daughter of Abraham and one of God's chosen people. She believed in the one, true, living God. Because of her relationship with Jesus, Mary is the ideal personification of her people Israel. That is, she is everything God wants his chosen people to be.

It's debatable, but tradition holds that Mary was from the predominant tribe of Judah, the patriarch called "lion" by his father Jacob (a.k.a. Israel). Some scholars think that Mary was also a descendant of the great King David, who united the Israelites and made them a great nation. That is why she has a place on the "Jesse tree," which is the Messiah's family tree, named for King David's father, Jesse. While Mary might have been royalty, however, she was far removed from living like any queen on earth. She lived humbly in the Promised Land that God gave her people. Today we also call it the Holy Land, because of her son.

The Government

In Mary's day, Palestine was occupied by Rome, a cruel oppressor that taxed the people and squelched rebellions violently. She could not have foreseen that one day her son would be executed by the Romans, not for violent rebellion but for preaching love and forgiveness. Ultimately, however, Jesus triumphed: Rome, once the heart of the Roman Empire, is now the seat of Jesus' Church.

Roman soldiers were everywhere in Palestine at the time. They could demand anything from the Jews and force them to serve them. Galilee, where

trivial tidbit...

Mary is called the flowering root of Jesse because of this messianic prophecy: "A shoot shall come out from the stump of Jesse, and a branch shall grow out of his root" (Isaiah 11:1).

Holy Land site...

The Synagogue Church, now in a busy market district of Nazareth, is believed to have been the synagogue where the Holy Family gathered for services with other Jews and where Jesus studied.

Jesus, Mary and Joseph lived, was a hotbed of hatred for Rome and therefore the home of rebels. During the Jewish uprisings around 6 A.D., just four miles from Nazareth, Roman soldiers burned the city of Sepphoris to the ground and sold its inhabitants into slavery. Possibly Mary saw some of the 2,000 men crucified along the roadside for attempted insurrection. Maybe her family helped hide the guerillas or at least fed them as they passed through Nazareth. Eventually, in 70 A.D., Rome would totally destroy the capital city of Jerusalem and the Temple.

When Mary was a child, Herod the Great was appointed by the emperor Augustus Caesar (Octavian) to rule Palestine. With taxes raised from the Jewish people, Herod built magnificent structures, including the Jewish Temple in Jerusalem, with its marble-covered courtyards and domes and walls plated with gold and silver. After Herod died in 4 B.C., his territory was divided among his three sons. Herod Antipas inherited Galilee and Herod Archelaus received Judea. Jews had to pay taxes to Rome and to Herod, as well as to the Temple.

Religion

Mary was steeped in Jewish tradition. Her life centered around prayer and the Jewish feasts. She observed Jewish rules and customs, such as those concerning the Sabbath, when thirty-nine types of work were forbidden—including lighting a fire, tying or untying a rope, and wearing hair ornaments.

Mary took ritual baths, called *mikvahs*, in special pools of well water, spring water, or rain water. These baths, in which the entire body was immersed, were required before entering the Temple to purify oneself after coming in contact with the dead, blood, or something unclean. Jewish women took these baths after their periods, before their weddings, and after childbirth. Likewise Mary would have observed the Jewish laws for hand washing before meals.

On the Sabbath (Saturday), Mary went to the synagogue, "the gathering place," in Nazareth. There in the area for women and children she listened to the men read Scripture, teach and discuss. She would prepare food the day before, because no work was to be done on the Sabbath, and would keep the Sabbath lamp burning at home.

For the three main festivals when Jews tried to travel to the Temple in Jerusalem—Passover, Pentecost and Tabernacles—Mary might have accompanied her parents and then later her husband and son. The Temple was the only place where animals were sacrificed. Morning and evening services, prayers, sermons, and discussions were held there. This Temple was built during Mary's lifetime. Perhaps she attended its dedication with her family in 10 B.C.

Mary was familiar with the stories of the patriarchs and other Hebrew heroes. Her heart thrilled to hear how God led her people out of slavery in Egypt to the Promised Land, and she trustingly waited for the Messiah to come and set her people free once again. Mary was one of the *anawim*, the simple, faithful people called the "poor of Yahweh," who waited in hope for God's kingdom. Eventually, for Christians all the expectations of Israel would be realized through her son.

Like all Jewish men and women, three times every day Mary prayed the eighteen benedictions, standing and facing the Temple. And, of course, Mary prayed the psalms, which were the Jewish song-prayers in Scripture. She probably knew many of them by heart. Imagine the quiet joy that flood-

big book search...

Certain Old Testament women prefigure, or foreshadow, Mary. Esther, a queen married to a Persian king, risked her life in order to save her Jewish people. Judith used cunning and her beauty to infiltrate the Assyrian army and cut off the head of its general, saving her people. Sarah, Miriam, Deborah and Ruth are other strong Hebrew women who preceded Mary in salvation history.

trivial tidbit...

The Church praises Mary in the words the Israelites greeted Judith with after her victory over the Assyrians: "You are the glory of Jerusalem, you are the great boast of Israel, you are the great pride of our nation!" (Judith 15:9)

All that stands of the Temple of Jerusalem today is part of the outer Western wall. One block alone is forty-six feet wide and weighs over four hundred tons. This wall is a primary holy place for Jews. They come from all over the world to pray there and mourn the loss of Jerusalem. For this reason the wall is called the Wailing Wall. Visitors (men on one side, women on the other) insert prayers on paper in the crevices between its stones. When leaving the wall, visitors don't turn their backs to it but walk away facing forward.

Feasts Mary Celebrated

Mary and her family celebrated the same feasts that Jewish people do today:

- ❖ **Passover**: a remembrance of the Hebrews' escape from Egypt
- ❖ **Pentecost**: celebrating God giving the law to Moses
- ❖ **Rosh Hashanah**: the Jewish New Year
- ❖ **Yom Kippur**: the Day of Atonement
- ❖ **Sukkoth (Tabernacles)**: recalling the huts the Hebrews lived in during the Exodus
- ❖ **Hanukkah**: in memory of the rededication of the Temple under the Maccabees
- ❖ **Purim**: a reminder of Esther's deliverance of the Jews

ed her heart when she prayed them after the Annunciation and the Nativity with new understanding and appreciation. The verses containing prophecies about the coming of the Messiah, however, would both console and alarm her, because they describe a king, the son of David, who would suffer.

Betrothal to Joseph

Jewish girls became marriageable at the age of twelve and a half. According to custom, when Mary was about that age, a man came to her father, Joachim, and arranged to have her betrothed to his son, named Joseph, from the tribe of Judah. In a ceremony, Joseph's father presented Joachim with a gift (the *mohar* or bride price) in exchange for Mary. This was required by law. Joseph himself also could have given Mary a gift as a token of his love. In turn, Joachim would provide a dowry for Mary, such as clothing or household furnishings. After this betrothal, the couple was considered as good as married, except that they did not yet live together. Ordinarily they would not be married for another year.

Joseph was a hardworking carpenter, a craft that might have put him a step above an ordinary laborer but not one that would have made him rich. He could have been about twenty-five years old, the ordinary age for Jewish men to marry, although some non-biblical stories and pieces of art have him as an older man, perhaps even a widower, which is plausible in view of the many women who died in childbirth back then. Chances are that Mary knew Joseph, since Nazareth was such a small town. And since Joseph undoubtedly had a reputation for being a man of integrity, Mary was surely pleased at the prospect of being his wife.

There's a non-biblical tradition that Mary had made a vow of perpetual virginity as a young girl. If so, betrothal to Joseph would have presented quite a predicament. Those who believe this tradition argue that Joseph too had made a vow of virginity or that Mary left it up to God to work it out or that when Mary disclosed her vow to Joseph he agreed to live with her as brother and sister. This story may have grown out of the early and medieval Church's high regard for virginity, and scholars today do not put much stock in it. They point out that to Jews at the time, marriage was expected and children were considered a great blessing, and so a vow of virginity would not have been understood or acceptable to Mary or her extended family. Besides, Mary would have needed her father's permission to make such a vow, and there is no hint of that anywhere.

Regardless, Mary's betrothal to Joseph set the stage for the greatest event to befall her people: the coming of their long-awaited Messiah.

THE WORD
WAS MADE FLESH

Spouse of the Holy Spirit
God's Message

Mary's life did not go as she might have planned. She would not live out her life as an average woman in a small town at the edges of the Roman Empire. Instead, she became the most famous and powerful woman in history, prayed to more often than any other human being other than her son and depicted in at least as many pieces of art as he has been. All this came from her simple *fiat* (Latin for "let it be") in response to God's will.

One day God revealed this young teenager's vocation to her through the message of an angel: She had been chosen to be the mother of the Messiah, who was the actual Son of God, the Word-made-flesh who would dwell among us. He would be called "Emmanuel," or "God with us."

We suppose that God could have saved the world some other way, but for some divine reason God decided to partner with this particular woman in a miraculous way. Mary would be both virgin and mother. She would conceive Jesus not through a man but through the Holy Spirit, so that it would be clear that Jesus descended directly from God. But it is also clear that Mary had a free choice in this decision. She could say yes as she did and allow God to be born into this world, but she also had the ability to say no.

The Annunciation (Luke 1:26-38)

We find the story of the Annunciation—the announcement of the conception of the Lord—in the first chapter of the Gospel of Luke. He tells the story with hindsight after the Resurrection and cleverly weaves it with Old

Consider a time when
you have said yes to
God as Mary did. Or
perhaps you said no.
Pray for the grace to
be open to God's will
and to answer God's
call whenever and
however it comes to
you.

Testament themes.

Scripture doesn't say what Mary was doing when God's messenger, the Angel Gabriel, came to her. One legend proposes that she was spinning, another that she was at the well. In any case, the awesome archangel appeared in the guise of a young man and spoke to her: "Hail, favored one. The Lord is with you." The Greek for the word *hail* is more accurately translated "rejoice," in fact, "rejoice greatly."

At this greeting, Mary must have drawn back in fear, eyes wide, heart stopped. For one thing, strange men didn't speak to women back then. What could this one's words of praise mean? Gabriel calmed her, "Do not be afraid, Mary, for you have found favor with God." How comforting for Mary to hear the angel call her familiarly by name and then to hear that she was pleasing to God. This phrase puts her in the class with other great people that Hebrew Scripture described as "having found favor" with God: Noah, Abraham, Moses and David all were called for a weighty task and assured of God's assistance.

Then the angel broke the news. "You will conceive and bear a son. You will name him Jesus. He will be great and will be called the Son of the Most High." The angel went on to say that God would give Jesus the throne of his ancestor David and his kingdom would last forever. Puzzled, Mary asked a practical question: "How can this be, since I am a virgin?" Gabriel explained that the Holy Spirit would come upon her, the power of God would overshadow her, and her child would be holy and called the Son of God. The Book of Genesis states that the Holy Spirit hovered over the waters and creation came forth. Now the Holy Spirit would bring forth a new creation through this young woman. Mary thus became the first person to hear the Gospel, the good news of the Savior. It took great faith for her to believe the angel's words.

The fate of the world hung on the young girl's assent. Some have mused that at that moment all the angels in heaven must have held their breath. Would Mary give God the gift of her humanity or not? Would her answer be "yes" or "no" or "not right now." They needn't have worried. Mary, the listening virgin, was always attuned to God's will and God's timetable. As St. Augustine put it, "Mary had first conceived the Lord in her mind, before she conceived him in her womb." Love made her vulnerable and fertile and fruitful, all at the same time.

Without a moment's hesitation—not asking for at least a day to think it over—and with tremendous courage, Mary gave the only answer she could, "Here am I, the servant of the Lord; let it be with me according to your word." The original Greek word was closer to "slave" than "servant." Mary offered herself to God without reservation, just as Jesus would some thirty or so years later. Like mother, like son! Praying in the Garden of Gethsemane the night before he died, Jesus echoed Mary's words and said to his Father, "Not my will but yours be done." He too was open to God's plan of salvation, just as his mother had been. With Mary's "Let it be," the course of history for the whole human family changed, and for this we are all indebted to her.

Because Mary put herself totally at God's disposal, she enabled God to redeem the entire human race, including herself. At Mary's yes, instantly the paradox of her virgin motherhood occurred. The God-man began to take shape in her. In the words of St. Gregory of Nyssa, the first time God took dust from the earth and formed man. The second time God took dust from the Virgin and formed man around himself. In this same moment Mary became

The knot tied by Eve's disobedience was untied by the obedience of Mary.

—St. Irenaeus

In Nazareth today stands the majestic basilica of the Annunciation, believed to be built over the site where the Annunciation occurred. In a crypt under the church there is a place marked in Latin, "Here the Word was made flesh." In the church there are images of Mary from many different countries. That of the United States depicts the glorious woman in the Book of Revelation. Mary is a graceful figure of shiny steel against a background of vivid, warm colors.

Favorite Marian Songs

❖ Ave Maria
❖ O Sanctissima (O Most Holy One)
❖ Immaculate Mary
❖ Hail, Holy Queen, Enthroned Above
❖ Gentle Woman
❖ On This Day, O Beautiful Mother
❖ Lo, How a Rose E'er Blooming
❖ What Child Is This?
❖ Daily, Daily, Sing to Mary

the mother of us all, who are the brothers and sisters of her son and thus the children of God.

St. Catherine of Siena pointed out in a poem how God respected Mary's freedom. She said to Mary, "Until you had agreed, the Son of God would not come down into your womb. He waited at the door of your will for you to open it." At the Annunciation, Mary was not just a puppet manipulated by God. No. Mary was a free, responsible woman who chose to cooperate with God, daring to take a risk and suffer the consequences. She couldn't have foreseen all that her "yes" would entail: Not only did she become a woman pregnant out of wedlock—a dangerous thing to be in her culture—but also she had to endure the pain of watching her son be crucified in front of her.

Mary's total self-offering the day the angel came sprang from her deep love for God. She made a commitment to God that day that she would remain faithful forever. At times we are urged by a voice within to make a positive change in our lives—to marry a certain person, to accept a new job, to take a stand on an issue, to undertake a mission, or to form a good habit. It takes courage and trust in God's goodness and provident care to act.

Mary demonstrated how to gracefully make the leap of faith into the dark unknown.

Then the angel left. Gabriel gave Mary no further information, instructions, or words of encouragement. There was no manual for her to follow. She probably didn't sleep a wink that night, wondering at the mystery of it all and the daunting task that lay before her. Of course, Mary didn't understand what was happening to her, but she trusted God to work it out. So in this way Mary was the first believer in the Good News, the first Christian. Her faith grew as ours does. Perhaps even she didn't fully realize who her son was until after the Resurrection.

The Incarnation

At Mary's "yes," almighty God, the God of Abraham and Moses and David, was able to become a human being. In the sonnet "The Mother of God in Glory," the nineteenth-century poet August Wilhelm Schlegel says to Mary, "The eternal love that bears the universe is unceasingly wedded to us through you." God's decision to enter the world through Mary was a wise one, for it made God more real, more accessible, more understandable to us humans. As the Jesuit theologian Karl Rahner put it, "Abstractions have no need of mothers."

In Mary's womb, Jesus drew his flesh and blood, his human life from her. Because Catholics believe that no man shared in Jesus' conception, all of his DNA, all of his human traits, must have been derived from Mary alone. In effect, Jesus was more like his mother than any son has ever been. He must have looked like her—maybe had her eyes and her smile—and probably took on many of her expressions and mannerisms. In the poem "Star of the Sea—Greetings to Mary" the eighteenth-century poet Clemens Brentano went so far as to declare,

In fables, the unicorn is only tamed and therefore able to be captured when it is in the presence of a virgin. Christians therefore came to view the unicorn as a symbol of Christ, with Mary as the virgin.

"He drank from your breasts; he sucked in your gentleness." Additionally, as Mary watched over the growth of the God-man and raised him, her qualities and virtues—along with those of Joseph—formed Jesus and helped make him the man he became.

A lovely poem expresses well through imagery the relationship between Mary and her son:

Mary the dawn, Christ the perfect day.
Mary the gate, Christ the heavenly way.
Mary the root, Christ the mystic vine.
Mary the grape, Christ the sacred wine
Mary the wheat sheaf, Christ the living bread.
Mary the rose tree, Christ the rose blood-red.
Mary the fount, Christ the cleansing flood.
Mary the chalice, Christ the saving blood.
Mary the beacon, Christ the haven's rest.
Mary the mirror, Christ the vision blest.
—Source unknown

What the Incarnation means more than anything else is that there is no longer a gulf between God and humankind. God is one of us and knows what it is like to be a mortal being. When "the Word became flesh and lived among us" (John 1:14), the divine spirit transformed the physical world. There is no more dualism, no more "us" and "God," no more "spiritual" and "material," no more "sacred" and "secular." We have Mary to thank for allowing that to happen.

The Virgin Mary

The French poet Rutebeuf wrote a hymn comparing God's transforming the virgin, Mary, into his mother to the sun passing through a windowpane without harming it. Her child was conceived not though sexual intercourse but through a direct act of God. This isn't so hard to believe when you consider that it is one aspect of a much larger miracle: that God became one of us in the first place. God had paved the way for this miraculous conception by having the barren Elizabeth, the relative of Mary, conceive in her old age. And before her, Sarah, the aged wife of Abraham—the first to believe in the one God—bore him a son when he was one hundred years old!

With Mary, the concept of virginity as an expression of total consecration to the Lord was introduced to the world. (The idea was foreign to the Jews, except for a Jewish sect in Egypt that had convents for "aged virgins.") The vowed virgin can have a special, intense love for the Lord that is not shared with anyone else. She or he can offer an undivided heart and belong body and soul to God. Caryll Houselander in *The Reed of God* offers three beautiful images of Mary's virginity as emptiness. She compares it to the hollow reed waiting to be filled with the breath of God to create lovely music, to a cup shaped to be filled with water or wine, and to a nest prepared as a warm, round ring to receive new life.

Catholics also believe that Jesus was an only child, despite the fact that in the Gospels four men (James, Joses, Judas and Simon) and two women (unnamed) are referred to as his "brothers and sisters." These could have been cousins, Joseph's children from a previous marriage, or other close relatives, but there is no way of knowing for sure, although if Jesus had siblings why did he need to entrust his mother to John, the beloved disciple? Again, the main point of the Annunciation story is that the birth of Jesus was a miraculous intervention of God in history and that "by the power of the Holy Spirit he was born of the virgin Mary and became man," as we say in the Nicene Creed. Was Mary a virgin? Catholics believe so, and thus we

Behold the power of the Virgin Mother. She wounded and took captive the heart of God.

—St. Bernardine of Siena

37

Catholics believe that Mary already appears in the first book of Scripture. After Adam and Eve sin, God speaks to the serpent (Satan) saying, "I will put enmity between you and the woman, and between your offspring and hers; he will strike your head, and you will strike his heel (Genesis 3:15)." In this promise of God, the woman is Mary, whose offspring, Jesus, crushes evil.

proudly call her the Virgin Mary.

There is more to being a virgin than just the physical aspect, however. It has overtones of strength and independence. A virgin woman stands alone, free to develop her own powers, gifts and creativity without the help or hindrance of a man. Virginity is also a symbol of the kingdom of God, where we will be dependent on and totally united with God. Because Mary is both virgin and mother and has lived as a single woman, wife, and widow, all women potentially can identify with and feel close to her as their sister, another daughter of Eve.

Christbearer
Errand of Mercy

The Incarnation wasn't all the stunning news contained in the Annunciation. Gabriel told Mary about another miracle in the family: Her barren relative Elizabeth, who was too old to have children, was already in her sixth month of pregnancy. How could this be, Mary wanted to know, and Gabriel provided the answer: "Nothing will be impossible with God" (Luke 1:37). It would be perfectly understandable if Mary had shut herself in her house and spent nine months simply wondering at the marvel the Lord had done and taking very good care of herself and the baby growing within her. That, however, was not like this remarkable young woman. She took Jesus, within her, out onto the streets and highways of the world. Mary's compassionate heart impelled her to travel to her relative Elizabeth to assist in the older woman's last three months of pregnancy. This was despite the fact that if Mary was like most pregnant women, she would have been experiencing morning sickness during her first trimester.

There are several possible motives for Mary's action. It would be difficult for Elizabeth to do the household chores while she was with child. So Mary went—"in haste" the Gospel says—to be with her in her time of need. Another motive might have been Mary's desire to share her own joy and concerns about her pregnancy with someone who was family and was pregnant as well. It has also been suggested that Mary made the journey in order to confirm the angel's words to her and thereby assure herself that she wasn't dreaming. This theory, however, doesn't mesh with Mary's chief virtue of faith. In any case, Mary again shows herself to be a decisive and gutsy young woman.

The Visit of Mary to Elizabeth (Luke 1:39-56)

Scripture doesn't name the town where Elizabeth lived but merely identifies it as a town in the hill country of Judea. Traditionally it is thought to be Ain Karem. The journey south from Nazareth to Judea was no easy undertaking, and Mary possibly had to do a lot of fast talking to persuade Joseph and her parents to let her go. Perhaps Joseph even went with her or sent a trusted friend or relative to accompany Mary.

Ain Karem was a few miles from Jerusalem, at least a three-day trip from Nazareth. The way was hot, stony, and sometimes uphill, not to mention dangerous because of the bandits who preyed on travelers. Although Mary and her companion probably joined a caravan of people heading in that direction, the trip required a lot of courage. Imagine what it was like for a pregnant, teenaged girl to travel among strangers, staying overnight at strange inns. The journey, however, did allow her time to reflect on the recent mysteries in her life.

Finally Mary came to the town and located the house of the Jewish priest Zechariah and his wife Elizabeth, either because she had visited them before with her family or because she simply asked for directions. While not as tiny as Nazareth, Ain Karem would still have been a relatively small town; and everyone would have known Zechariah because of his connection with the Temple in Jerusalem.

Mary probably walked through the open door of the house unannounced and greeted Elizabeth. Since there were no phones or Internet in those days, her "Visitation" as we call it most likely was a surprise. Elizabeth was startled to hear Mary's voice. Moreover, the boy she was carrying in her womb leapt at the sound. He was the future John the Bap-

Today on the top of a hill in Ain Karem (which means "spring of the vineyard") stands the beautiful Church of the Visitation, supposedly built on the site of the house of Elizabeth and Zechariah. Climbing the steep, rugged hill gives pilgrims a taste of Mary's experience. The church's cream-colored stone gleams in the sun. On the front, a large mosaic shows Mary coming to the town seated on a donkey. Inside the church is a large fresco of Mary and Elizabeth embracing under the rays of the Holy Spirit in the form of a dove. The courtyard walls display the Magnificat lettered in forty-one languages.

tist, who would someday baptize Mary's son, preach to prepare people for Jesus' coming, and eventually be beheaded for calling King Herod to repent. John seemed to recognize the presence of the Messiah within Mary. Elizabeth, through the inspiration of the Holy Spirit, certainly did. She greeted Mary with a loud voice, saying, "Most blessed are you among women, and blessed is the fruit of your womb." And she asked, "How is it that the mother of my Lord should come to me?" With this, Elizabeth became the first to acknowledge and venerate Mary as the Mother of God.

Elizabeth let Mary know that her baby leapt inside her for joy. Then she praised her young relative by saying, "Blessed are you who believed that what was spoken to you by the Lord would be fulfilled." How happy and relieved Mary was to hear Elizabeth's words. They confirmed that she wasn't just dreaming or imagining what had happened to her.

Mary is called "blessed" here because of her faith in God. Of all her virtues, faith is pre-eminent. She listened to God, believed, assented and then acted in accordance with God's plan. That is the very definition of a faithful Christian.

Mary's Song of Salvation (Luke 1: 46-55)

The response to Elizabeth that Luke puts on Mary's lips is a passionate canticle woven with verses and themes of the Old Testament. We call Mary's prayer-song the Magnificat from its opening words in Latin: *"Magnificat anima mea Dominum"* ("My soul magnifies the Lord"). The first four verses are a burst of praise for God in which Mary extols the Lord for what he has done for her. She declares herself his handmaid and frankly (and correctly) predicts that all ages would call her "blessed." Yet Mary humbly acknowledges that all her graces were free

trivial tidbit...

The Magnificat may have been one of the first Christian hymns. Today it is prayed every day as part of the evening prayer of the Liturgy of the Hours, the official prayer of the Church, which is said by all monks and many others.

big book search...

Read for yourself the complete Magnificat in Luke 1:46-55 or on pages 153-154 of this book.

gifts from God.

The rest of the prayer describes God's mercy to believers in politically radical terms: God acts to bring down the proud and mighty, feed the hungry, and raise the poor and lowly. In the end Mary recalls God's mercy to her people, the descendants of Abraham. As Mary sings this canticle, she represents her people Israel, who longed for freedom. She also sings for the Church, which longs for the establishment of the reign of God—the reign of peace and justice—"on earth as it is in heaven," as her son would later teach us to pray.

The Magnificat praises God for liberating people. The brave young woman who sang this victory song was instrumental in freeing all of humanity from slavery to sin and fear. Later Jesus described his mission in words that mirror the Magnificat: "He has anointed me to bring good news to the poor. He has sent me to proclaim release to the captives and recovery of sight to the blind, to let the oppressed go free" (Luke 4:18). Both Mary and Jesus stand shoulder to shoulder with those who work for freedom and justice for all.

The Chariot of Fire

Scripture says that Mary stayed with Elizabeth about three months. During those weeks Mary would have done the household chores for Elizabeth and her husband Zechariah such as shopping, fetching water, cooking, and doing laundry. Perhaps she sewed baby clothes for her child and that of Elizabeth. If Mary had morning sickness, Elizabeth would have comforted her.

Zechariah was mute during this entire visit because of his lack of faith when the angel had announced John's birth to him, but Mary and Elizabeth certainly delighted in each other's company, sharing their joy in their pregnancies and planning how they would care for their sons.

Mary's visit would have extended to the time Elizabeth gave birth. It makes sense that Mary was present for John's birth and even assisted at it, although Luke doesn't state this explicitly. Mary's return home was even more arduous than her journey to Ain Karem, for now she was at least three months pregnant. She also had to face the reactions of her townspeople—and her husband—to her unexplained (and unexplainable) pregnancy.

Mary in this story brings Christ to others. She not only brings him physically, but extends Christ-like mercy and love to her extended family. St. Catherine of Siena called Mary "the chariot of fire." That fire is nothing less than the burning love of God.

big book search...

Look up 1 Samuel 2:1–10. This prayer, very similar to the Magnificat, was prayed by Hannah, the mother of Samuel, the Jewish priest and prophet. Like Mary, Hannah was expressing gratitude to God for sending her a son miraculously, because she had been barren.

Blessed Virgin
Marriage to Joseph

What did Mary say when the angel asked her to be God's mother?" In answer to this question on a religion test, one eighth-grade student wrote: "Why me?" Mary did not respond that way, but surely a thousand questions filled her mind when the angel appeared to her.

Not the least of Mary's concerns would have been about how the man to whom she was betrothed would react. What would he say and do? First of all, Joseph would have known that the child was not his. The only logical assumption was that it was some other man's. Certainly it would have been impossible for him to even imagine the real situation.

Yet this must have confused Joseph to no end. After all, he knew what kind of good, pious young woman Mary was, and he couldn't have believed easily that she would have been unfaithful to him. Besides, even if he were furious with her he wouldn't necessarily have wanted to see her disgraced or harmed. He knew that if he divorced Mary for adultery, she might well be stoned to death.

Scripture doesn't say whether Mary informed Joseph that she was pregnant or just let him realize it from observing her. Neither does it say whether Mary disclosed to him that God was the father of her child. Poor Joseph. He must have been deeply in love with Mary and left in a quandary: What should he do? Many feel that Joseph must have talked with Mary about her condition and learned her sacred secret directly from her. This is the most likely scenario, given the holiness of these two great saints. Even so, Joseph must have felt awe and humility. He might have thought he was not worthy to become her spouse under the circumstances. In any case,

big book
search...

The Book of Proverbs 31:10–31, often called "Ode to a Capable Wife," describes the accomplishments and the perfections of an ideal married woman. It also provides a verbal portrait of the valiant Mary as she carried out her mission of wife and mother in Nazareth.

Joseph faced a dilemma that no other man—before or since—has had to face.

As for the people in Nazareth, they could have assumed that Joseph and Mary had sexual relations during their betrothal period, which wasn't all that unusual for young couples of the time and would not have been considered all that scandalous. Or they might have heard or even spread rumors that Mary had broken her vows to Joseph. What Mary's parents, Joachim and Anne, thought is not recorded anywhere. One thing is certain: Mary and Joseph had a real problem.

Good News for Joseph (Matthew 1:18-25)

The first chapter of the Gospel of Matthew tells Joseph's side of the story—what can be called the "Annunciation to Joseph." We have no idea how long Joseph endured the anguish caused by Mary's situation, but just when Joseph had decided to divorce Mary quietly and avoid publicly disgracing her, God stepped in.

While Joseph was asleep, an angel, most likely Gabriel again, appeared to him. The angel addressed him as "Joseph, son of David" and told him not to be afraid to take Mary as his wife, for the child was from the Holy Spirit. Gabriel foretold that Mary would have a son. Moreover, he instructed Joseph to name the boy Jesus, which means "God saves," because he would save people from their sins. Then, according to Matthew, the angel explained that this was happening to fulfill the prophecy: "Look the virgin shall conceive and bear a son, and they shall name him Emmanuel, which means, 'God is with us.'" This quotation is from Isaiah, where the original word for "virgin" simply means "young girl."

So, his fears allayed by the message of the angel,

fyi...

Since Joseph provided housing for the Holy Family, people look to him for help when they are trying to sell their house. Today it is a custom not only among Catholics to bury a statue of St. Joseph upside down in the yard in hopes that he will intercede for the sellers. When the house sells, they retrieve the statue and set it in a place of honor in their new house. A key to whether this is a superstition or a genuine devotion is whether or not the statue of Joseph is dug up after the house sells and returned to a place of honor inside the home.

Joseph embarked on his mission of service. Cutting the betrothal year short, he proceeded to wed Mary and assumed his role of protector of both the child and his mother. It's been surmised that Joseph too was a virgin his entire life. That is why in some art he is shown with a lily, the symbol of purity. We'll never know what this gentle man thought about all this, but we can deduce from the way that his son "increased in wisdom and in years, and in divine and human favor" (Luke 2:52) that Joseph was a good husband and father. So good, in fact, that when Jesus was looking for a way to refer to God, he could come up with no better word than "Abba" or "Daddy," which is what he would have called Joseph as well.

In those days, lineage was traced through the father. Since Joseph was of the House of David, Jesus was regarded as the son of David too. The genealogy that Matthew provides for Jesus (Matthew a cool website...

Go to www.saint joseph.org and click on "English" in the upper right-hand corner to learn more about St. Joseph. This site includes information about the Oratory of St. Joseph of Mount Royal, the largest church in Canada and the largest pilgrimage site for St. Joseph in the world. The basilica was the dream of Brother André Bessette, a simple, humble member of the Congregation of the Holy Cross, who was beatified in 1982.

1:1–16), however, includes four women: Tamar, Rahab, Ruth and Bathsheba (the wife of Uriah). Each of these women was a sinner or a foreigner who entered the family tree of the Messiah in an unusual way. After her husband died and her father-in-law did not provide for her to have a child as the law said, Tamar tricked him into impregnating her. Rahab was a prostitute who helped the Israelites gain the Promised Land. Ruth was a Gentile who snagged Boaz as a husband with the help of her first mother-in-law, Naomi. Bathsheba committed adultery with King David, who then had her husband killed. Despite their unusual actions, these women paved the way for the coming of the Savior, as did Mary, who gave birth to that Savior in an extraordinary manner. The genealogy concludes, "Jacob, the father of Joseph, the husband of Mary, of whom Jesus was born, who is called the Messiah."

Joseph had the name of the son of Jacob, the owner of the "coat of many colors" who had been sold into slavery by his jealous brothers. Later, that same Joseph became the astute leader in Egypt who saved his brethren and the entire world from famine. St. Joseph likewise took good care of Jesus—even taking Mary and him into that same Egypt to escape King Herod. And in a way, by saving "the Bread of Life" from harm, Joseph too fed the entire world. Coincidentally, dreams played a role in the lives of both Josephs. The Old Testament Joseph had prophetic dreams and was an interpreter of dreams. The New Testament Joseph was guided by God through his dreams.

Nowhere in Scripture does Joseph ever speak. Yet this silent man was the one responsible for teaching Jesus the Jewish religion and for being the strength and protector of the most precious woman in the world. In Matthew's Gospel, Joseph is called a "righteous man." Like Mary, he was chosen to play a special role in the salvation of the world. Therefore, after her, St. Joseph is often regarded as the greatest saint in the Church. We celebrate two days in his honor: March 19 and May 1, the feast of St. Joseph the Worker. He is the patron saint of both Italy and Poland, as well as the patron saint of fathers and husbands.

Joseph carried out his mission so well that he received the title of patron of the universal Church. Just as he once cared for Jesus, he now watches over the Church, the people who comprise the Mystical Body of Christ.

The Wedding and Marriage

The wedding of Mary and Joseph might have been toned down in view of the circumstances and the haste. Ordinarily, however, Jewish weddings were grand affairs that could last seven days. Mary might have made the traditional wedding gifts for her groom: a prayer shawl and a shroud. She also could have made her wedding dress and embroidered it with lovely patterns. She would have worn a headdress highly decorated with ornaments and maybe even silver coins. And she would have been perfumed with the rich fragrances of the East.

On the evening of the first day, the groom, also wearing a crown, came to the bride's house and escorted her in a procession to his house, guided along the way by lights held by attendants. At Joseph's house, which perhaps he built himself, the wedding blessing was given. Wedding rings weren't exchanged, for this was not the custom. The guests then enjoyed wonderful food, music and dancing—with the men and women dancing separately. Both Mary and Joseph must have rejoiced in a special way, since their "public relations" crisis—not to

trivial tidbit...

Early anti-Christian propaganda claimed that Mary's child was illegitimate, the son of a Roman soldier named Panthera, who had raped her. There is no historical basis for this slander and certainly no place for it for those who believe the Scriptures.

Holy Land site...

Ten minutes away from the Basilica of the Annunciation in Nazareth is St. Joseph Church, marking the traditional site of Joseph's carpentry shop.

49

mention their first marital crisis—had been averted.

After their wedding, Mary and Joseph must have had an intimate relationship. We can say this with confidence because even if their marriage was not consummated in a physical sense their family is held up by the Church as a model for family life as "The Holy Family." This means that it was full of love and respect and fruitfulness. For this family raised the divine child whom we recognize as "the way, the truth, and the life" (John 14:6). Mary and Joseph shared something wonderful in common: a starring role in the great mystery of redemption that allowed them to live under the same roof with God. What a concept!

As with any married woman, Mary must have experienced the give and take of living with a husband. She had to get used to Joseph's personality, opinions and quirks—and he with hers. With him, she grew in the art of compromise, sacrifice and love. In his love and self-sacrifice, she saw mirrored the love of God for her. If Joseph did indeed bring other children to the marriage, Mary also assumed the role of stepmother, which could have been challenging for one so young.

Watching Joseph as he worked with wood or as he lay sleeping in their little house, Mary had to be grateful that God provided such a good man to share the burden and the bliss of caring for the Savior of the world. Although we commonly call Joseph a carpenter, the word Scripture uses for his occupation is broader than that. It means builder or construction worker. Most likely Joseph made home furnishings and farm implements but also erected buildings. Joseph probably never dreamed that his marriage to Mary would make his life far more exciting than any small-town carpenter could ever expect.

Joseph must have died before Jesus left home to

begin his public life. We think this for two reasons. First of all, the Gospels say nothing about Joseph when telling about Jesus' public ministry. Second, because there were no last names, a man was usually identified as "the son of" followed by his father's name, but Jesus is sometimes referred to as the son of Mary, instead of the son of Joseph.

Unless Joseph died unexpectedly, such as in a construction accident, he either died of illness or old age. It must have been hard for Mary to watch as her beloved companion and protector grew weaker and more dependent on her and Jesus, gradually turning over the carpentry business to his son. We surmise that both Mary and Jesus were with Joseph when he died, and so he must have had a happy death. For this reason, Joseph is also known as the patron saint of a happy death. His passing, though, left Mary a widow and a single parent. If Joseph died before Jesus was not yet twenty years old, another male relative or appointed person would have become guardian of his widow and child. If Jesus was twenty or older, he would have become the legal head of the house. Because she was a woman, Mary would never have been considered the head of the house in her time.

Mother of God
Birth of Jesus

he earliest art we have of Mary is a fresco from the early third century on the wall of the catacomb of St. Priscilla in Rome. It shows Mary with the infant Jesus at her breast, while a man beside her points to a star above her head. This maternal depiction is appropriate, for the concept that Mary is the Mother of God is the foundation of everything else we believe about her. As Martin Luther dramatically put it, "No one can say anything greater about her or to her, even if he had as many tongues as there are leaves and grass, stars in the sky, or sand by the sea." All of Mary's special privileges flow from her pivotal role in salvation history: the human mother of God-become-a-human-being.

While Mary's child was growing up, no one ever guessed that his father was God, the almighty, the Yahweh of the Hebrews. How could they? The notion is simply beyond human comprehension. It is what we Catholics call "a mystery of faith." We do not have to understand it to believe it.

As Jesus' mother, Mary cared for, nurtured, and taught her boy like any other mother. She nursed the infant Jesus, burped him, changed his diapers, bathed him, tickled him, and rocked him to sleep by singing Jewish lullabies. Later she heard his first word—no doubt "Mama" (in Aramaic)—and watched him crawl and discover the world. She coaxed him into taking his first steps and potty-trained him. It was Mary to whom Jesus ran when he fell or lost a baby tooth. Intent on capturing the real motherhood that was Mary's, one artist portrayed her spanking a baby Jesus for some childhood transgression! It was under Mary's guidance and enveloped by her love that God learned what it was to be a human being.

In Bethlehem stands the Basilica of the Nativity, supposedly built over the place where Jesus was born. The doorway to the church is low, bricked in by the Crusaders to prevent invading Muslims on horseback from entering. How appropriate it is that one must bend low in order to gain access to this particular holy site. The stone steps lead to a cave, and in the floor is a star with glass in the center, marking the holy spot of Jesus' birth. East of Bethlehem is Shepherd's Field, where there is a church with frescos depicting the nativity events on its walls.

St. Ignatius and Our Lady

As a newly converted knight en route to the Holy Land, Ignatius decided to visit the popular shrine at Montserrat in Spain, where there was a Black Madonna. On the way he met a Moor, and they got into a discussion about Mary. The Moor argued against Mary's perpetual virginity. After they parted and Ignatius thought about it, he concluded that he had to defend Our Lady's honor. He would catch up to the Moor, capture him, and take him to the Shrine of Our Lady of Montserrat, where he would force him to honor her and then kill him. Not sure that this was the right thing to do, however, at the crossroads Ignatius let go of the reins and let the mule decide whether to take the road the Moor had followed or the narrower road to the shrine. The mule chose the road to the shrine, saving the Moor's life and Ignatius' eternal soul. At Montserrat, Ignatius made a commitment to his new life. He presented his mule to the monastery and gave up his sword and dagger, which was hung on the grille before Our Lady's statue. On the vigil of the Annunciation he gave his fine clothes to a poor man and put on the prickly garment of a pilgrim, which he wore for the rest of his life.

The Nativity (Luke 2:1-7)

The Gospel of Luke presents the portrait of the birth of Jesus that has inspired our celebrations of Christmas. It says that the Roman emperor, Caesar Augustus, decreed that a census be taken for which everyone in his empire had to register in the town of their families of origin. Because Joseph was from the house of David, he had to travel to Bethlehem, the city of David, which was in Judea, the southern province of Palestine.

Mary was in her ninth month of pregnancy, and it is uncertain whether as a woman she was obliged to participate in the census. Nevertheless, she packed up the necessary belongings for the journey and accompanied Joseph. Who knows why the couple would have made this decision, but it shows their devotion to each other. The trip to Bethlehem also made it possible for Jesus to be born in that "city of David," thereby fulfilling an Old Testament prophecy that the Messiah would be born there.

Mary and Joseph probably joined a caravan of other people traveling to Bethlehem, which was about ninety-five miles south of Nazareth. Although Christmas cards show Mary riding a donkey, more than likely she walked. In either case, it was quite a feat for a woman in the last weeks of pregnancy. On reaching Jerusalem, being devout Jews, the couple must have visited the Temple. The entire journey took at least four days, and by the time they arrived at Bethlehem Mary must have been exhausted and uncomfortable—not to mention as anxious as every young mother about to give birth for the first time.

Joseph tried to find a nice, private place for them to stay overnight, but so many people had flooded the town that there was "no room for them in the inn." No relatives took them in, which seems a little strange. Maybe they had heard of the "scandal" from other Nazarenes. The inns of the time were usually nothing more than open courtyards surrounded by small shelters that afforded minimal privacy, but these were full anyway. So Joseph brought Mary to a shelter for animals, probably a grotto or cave. There, sometime during their stay in Bethlehem, Mary, hardly more than a child herself, gave birth to the Son of God. It is a story worth repeating and celebrating every year.

We assume that Mary's mother and female rela-

The Roman emperor Caesar Augustus, who was regarded by many as the "savior of the world" and a god himself, began a long era of relative peace known as the *Pax Romana* or "Peace of Rome." It is ironic that during his reign Mary's son appeared, who was the true savior of the world, the Prince of Peace who brings true peace to earth.

big book search...

Read the prophecy about Bethlehem in Micah 5:1–4.

tives were not there to support and coach the first-time mother. The Gospels don't mention a midwife (although the apocryphal gospels mention one or two), so perhaps Joseph assisted in the delivery alone. It is hard for us to imagine this today, but it would not have been unheard of in those days. It was Mary, however, who wrapped the baby in swaddling clothes. These were bands of material that bound the infant's arms and legs to ensure that they would grow straight. Mary then placed the baby Jesus in a manger, which is a feedbox for the animals. How providential that Jesus, who called himself "the Bread of Life," would have been born in Bethlehem, a name that means "house of bread," and then was placed in a feedbox! Comparing Mary and Eve, St. Bernard of Clairvaux said, "Instead of the fruit of the tree of death, she offers to humankind the bread of life."

The Shepherds (Luke 2:8-20)

Mary and Joseph were the first to see the God-man and hear his cries. Any baby is a source of amazement, but this one must have been even more so to the two of them. God depended on this young woman and her new husband to keep Jesus alive and care for him. In effect, God surrendered himself to them. Again, this extraordinary mystery required great faith from both Mary and Joseph. They believed that Joseph held in his strong arms the omnipotent, eternal God and that Mary's lap was the throne for the King of the Universe.

A little while after the birth, shepherds appeared at the cave, out of breath and excited. Their job was to watch over sheep—perhaps including the lambs that were used in the Temple sacrifices. They had come to see the Lamb of God, and Mary and Joseph graciously received them. These simple, rough men,

Theotokos: Mother of God

During the first centuries after Jesus died, the Church had to work out ways of describing who he was. The early theologians, such as Ambrose, Athanasius, Augustine, Basil, Clement of Alexandria, Gregory of Nazianzus and Origen, hammered out the doctrines that we today take for granted. We believe that Jesus is fully divine and fully human, that he is the second person of the Trinity, that he is the Son of God.

When some bishops in the fifth century began teaching that Jesus was not really divine, a Church council of all bishops was called to clarify the issue. At this Council of Ephesus in 431, it was definitely decided by the Church that Jesus was both God and man, that he had two natures, one divine and one human.

Furthermore, the council reasoned, if this is true, then Mary must be the mother of God. The bishops called her *Theotokos* in Greek, or God-bearer. At the end of the council, St. Cyril of Alexandria prayed to Mary, greeting her as the "dwelling of him whom no dwelling can contain." This honor of being the mother of God set Mary above all creation in heaven and earth.

for your spiritual health...

Jesus grew inside of Mary for nine months. You, too, are a temple of God. That is, God is growing inside of you. During the next day or two, take a few moments to turn your attention within and address the God who dwells in you.

trivial tidbit...

The first Marian shrine in the United States is in St. Augustine, Florida. It is devoted to *Nuestra Señora de Leche y Buen Parto* (Our Lady of Milk and Good Birth) and houses a statue from the early seventeenth century by the same name.

who were considered the dregs of society and sinners (for they certainly didn't keep all the rules of the Jewish religion), told a fantastic story: That night, as they were watching their flocks, an angel stood before them and light shone around them, frightening them to death. The angel told them not to be afraid. He said, "I am bringing you good news of great joy for all the people. To you is born this day in the city of David a savior, who is the Messiah, the Lord. This will be a sign for you: you will find a child wrapped in bands of cloth and lying in a manger." Suddenly, the shepherds had a magnifi-

A legend holds that when Jesus was cold and fussing in the manger, a tabby cat nestled against him and soothed him with purring. In gratitude Mary placed an M on the cat's forehead that now appears on every tabby cat. (The only problem with this story is that the Latin "M" is not the Aramaic letter Mary would have used for her name!)

cent vision. A great number of angels appeared, all saying, "Glory to God in the highest heaven, and on earth peace among those whom he favors." Then the heavenly visitors disappeared.

The shepherds' words were engraved on Mary's heart. They were a precious gift to her, and over and over she thought about what the words meant. How characteristic of God to announce the Good News of the Savior first to a group of people who were poor and considered untrustworthy. Some day Mary's son would call himself "the good shepherd," who lays down his life for his sheep.

Our Birthing of Christ

The fourteenth-century Dominican preacher and mystic Meister Eckhart exhorted all to be Mother of God. He wrote, "What matters is that God should be born in me." When we were baptized, God entered our hearts and we too became full of grace. God, dwelling in us, asks us to bring him forth into the world. In this, Mary is our model.

Mary's whole life was centered on bearing and rearing Jesus. We too ought to make it our number one priority to nurture Christ's life in us and then share him with the world. Mary was courageous and daring to the point of foolishness in her pregnancy. How much do we risk in promoting Christ and his Gospel message? Mary remained steadfast to her calling and her convictions despite what others thought and said. Being true to our baptismal vows sometimes means living in a way that opens us to criticism, scorn and abuse. Finally, Mary went on blindly following her calling, trusting God to work things out. She inspires us to persevere in faith, living our Christian life confident that the divine power that overshadowed us is lovingly using us somehow to further God's great plan of salvation.

Daughter of Zion
Simeon's Prophecy

Eight days after Jesus was born, he was circumcised either at a synagogue or at home. This surgery was performed on all Jewish males as a sign of their special covenant and relationship with God. It inducted them into the Chosen People. We wonder what Mary's thoughts were as she saw her baby's blood shed for the first time. On this occasion, the baby was given his name. Both Mary and Joseph had been told by the angel that his name was to be Jesus. In Hebrew this was Joshua or Yeshua, a popular Jewish name that means "God saves." For almost six undisturbed weeks in Bethlehem, Mary had the ecstatic joy of being a young mother with a perfect baby boy. Then duty led her to a harsh awakening.

Mary was a true daughter of Zion (Jerusalem). She faithfully followed the religious laws of her people, even when we might think they didn't apply to her and her son. That is why forty days after the birth of Jesus, she and Joseph traveled to Jerusalem, which is six miles north of Bethlehem, taking Jesus to the Temple for the first time to consecrate him to God in a ritual known as "the Presentation." Firstborn sons were considered sacred to God, and Jews of the time were required to pay a priest five shekels of silver to "buy back" their firstborn sons. This practice had its origins in the Exodus story, in which the firstborn sons of the Israelites were not killed when the Angel of Death passed over Egypt.

In addition, a woman was to come to the Temple forty days after the birth of a son in order to be purified. Her contact with the blood of childbirth would have made her "unclean," that is, unfit for participating in religious ceremonies. Purification was achieved by bathing in the *mikvah* (rit-

The Presentation of
the Lord observed on
February 2 is also
called Candlemas
Day. Because Simeon
called Jesus the Light
for the Gentiles, the
Presentation began to
be celebrated with
candlelight proces-
sions. Today on this
feast candles for use
in the liturgy are
blessed at Mass.

short prayer...

*O Lady, by the love
which you bear Jesus,
help me to love him.*
        —St. Bridget

The Sorrows of Mary

Tradition lists seven sorrows that Mary had to endure:
1. The prophecy of Simeon (Luke 2:34–35)
2. The flight to Egypt (Matthew 2:13–22)
3. The loss of Jesus for three days (Luke 2:41–52)
4. The ascent to Calvary (John19:17)
5. The crucifixion and death of Jesus (Matthew 27:31–28:10; Mark 15; Luke 23;13–24:12; John 19–20)
6. Jesus taken down from the cross (John 19:39–40)
7. Jesus laid in the tomb (John 19:40–42)

ual water). Mary was also to sacrifice a lamb to make up for sins or, if she couldn't afford a lamb, two turtledoves or pigeons, one as a burnt-offering and the other as a sin offering, that is, to make up for sins. The Scriptures say that Joseph and Mary purchased a pair of birds, so we know that the Holy Family, who belonged to the working-class poor, was not well-to-do.

The Devout Simeon and Anna (Luke 2:22–38)

A good, faithful man named Simeon lived in Jerusalem. He was one of the *anawim* (faithful ones) who looked forward to a savior. It had been re-vealed to Simeon that he wouldn't die until he had seen the Messiah. The Spirit sent him to the Temple on the day the Holy Family came.

Despite all the couples bringing babies to the Temple, when the Holy Family entered, Simeon rec-ognized them. Then not only did he see the Messi-ah, but he was privileged to take the baby Jesus into his arms. Simeon prayed that God might let him go in peace now, for he had seen the salvation God had prepared. He described the child as a light to the Gentiles and the glory for God's people Israel.

Mary and Joseph were astonished at the old man's words about Jesus. His prayer served as a second annunciation, confirming and expanding the news of the Messiah delivered by the Angel Gabriel. Simeon blessed the couple, and then, speaking only to Mary, he uttered a disturbing prophecy. He said, "This child is destined for the falling and the rising of many in Israel, and to be a sign that will be opposed." He also said to Mary, "A sword will pierce your own soul too."

These words were a blow to the young couple. Now they knew that there were conflict and pain in store for their son and for Mary. This news hung over their lives like a dark cloud. As Mary held her infant in her arms, little did she guess that more than thirty years later she would again hold that same body—only this time it would be that of a man who had just been executed as a criminal.

At that moment Anna entered. She was an eighty-four-year old widow, a prophet who lived at the Temple, praying and fasting. Like Simeon, Anna was one of the *anawim*. She too recognized the Messiah and praised God. This was another affirmation for Mary that soothed her after Simeon's bad news. Then Anna began spreading the word about Jesus to all who were waiting for the Savior.

trivial tidbit...

Originally, Mount Zion was a mountain with a fortress near Jerusalem captured by King David. Now the term stands for both Israel and its capital Jerusalem.

fyi...

The prayer of Simeon is prayed every night in the Liturgy of the Hours.

Star of Evangelization
Visit of the Magi

A ccording to the Gospel of Matthew, Simeon's prophecy soon began to come true. King Herod, the highest authority in the land, was accidentally alerted that there might be a rival to his throne. An ambitious, ruthless man, Herod had killed his two sons and the favorite of his ten wives when he suspected them of plotting to take his throne. The Jews, for whom pigs were unclean animals, had a saying, "It's better to be Herod's pig than his son."

The Wise Men (Matthew 2:1-12)

By this time the Holy Family was living in a house in Bethlehem, probably a rented one. One night, *magi*—wise men or astronomers from the East—came to the door. Radiant with joy and awe, they knelt before the child Jesus, who was no doubt clinging to Mary his mother. Someone pointed out that as the magi knelt before Jesus they were also kneeling before Mary. Joseph isn't mentioned in the story.

Then the visitors opened the treasure chests they brought with them and gave Jesus expensive gifts: gold, frankincense and myrrh. (One cartoon mused that if there had been three wise women, the gifts would have been diapers, baby clothes, and formula!) We assume there were three magi because there were three gifts. There might have been more. The traditional names of the magi—Caspar, Melchior and Balthazar—are from a sixth-century Greek manuscript.

No doubt the wise men explained to the couple that in their country (probably Persia, present-day Iran) they had seen the rising of a new star

It is thought that the magi's kneeling before Jesus and Mary is the origin of the Christian practice of kneeling. The Jews and Romans did not kneel for prayer because they considered this posture too demeaning.

For insignts into the story of the magi, read *Starlight: Beholding the Christmas Miracle All Year Long* by John Shea (available at www. actapublications.com).

Our Lady of Aparecida

In the state of São Paulo in Brazil, the largest Catholic country, stands an enormous basilica in honor of Our Lady of Aparecida (Our Lady Who Appeared). Each year at least five million pilgrims visit the basilica; and October 12, the feast of Our Lady of Aparecida, attracts more than 200,000 people.

This devotion began in 1717 when, in preparation for the visit of a dignitary, three men went fishing. They caught nothing but a dark brown statue of the Immaculate Conception with the head missing. In another place they netted the head. After praying to Mary, the fisherman found their nets overflowing with fish.

The village treasured the statue, which had been made in 1650 by a monk and somehow had fallen into the river. Now the little black Madonna wears a richly embroidered mantle and a crown. It is said that once a runaway slave hid in the church where this statue was, and his shackles fell away, leading to the abolition of slavery in Brazil.

In 1931, Our Lady of Aparecida was proclaimed Queen and Patroness of Brazil. Children are named Aparecida, and the word is also used as an exclamation of surprise. Each year thousands walk miles to the basilica on a Pilgrimage of Those Without to protest on behalf of Brazil's poor and to call on Mary to aid those in need.

that signified the birth of a king. They had followed the star in search of the Messiah, the King of the Jews. In Jerusalem, when the magi had been asking people where the newborn king was, King Herod had summoned them. He asked them when the star was first seen. Then he sent them to Bethlehem with instructions to return when they found the new king, supposedly so that he too could do him homage. Actually Herod wanted to do away with this threat to his throne.

This visit by the Gentile foreigners must have been baffling but reassuring for Mary. Perhaps she recalled how Simeon had said that Jesus would be a light for the Gentiles. She was probably familiar, too, with the Old Testament prophecies:

May the kings of Tarshish and of the isles render him tribute, may the kings of Sheba and Seba bring gifts. May all kings fall down before him, all nations give him service (Psalms 72:10-11).

Nations shall come to your light, and kings.... The young camels of Midian and Ephah; all those from Sheba shall come. They shall bring gold and frankincense, and shall proclaim the praise of the Lord (Isaiah 60:1, 6).

Because these prophecies referred to kings and camels, the magi metamorphosed over the centuries into three "kings." Crowned and paying tribute to the King of Kings, they and their camels have become standard figures in our nativity sets.

Fortunately, the wise men dreamed that they were not to go back to Herod, so they returned home by another route. Mary and Joseph were probably glad to have the magi's expensive gifts for the next, unexpected stage of their lives.

Sister in the Faith
Escape into Egypt

ary and Joseph and Jesus were still in Bethlehem after the visit of the magi. Perhaps they had even planned to settle there for some reason. Or maybe they were merely postponing a return to Nazareth until any scandal over the child's birth had blown over. Or possibly Mary or Jesus could have been weak from the childbirth. In any case, Mary's journeying away from home was not over. Matthew's Gospel relates that one night Joseph woke her up with news as shocking as a sudden thunderclap. Imagine the expression of concern on Joseph's face as he relayed to a sleepy Mary that while he was sleeping an angel appeared to him in a dream that turned into a nightmare. The angel told Joseph that Herod was going to try to find Jesus to kill him. They were to flee to Egypt until further notice.

This would be Mary's fourth long journey in one year: the trips back and forth to visit Elizabeth, the journey to Bethlehem, and now and even longer journey to a foreign country—one that had been the land of slavery for the Hebrews before the Exodus. Facing this latest crisis, a lesser woman might have exclaimed, "Enough is enough." Mary might have cried (she was human, you know), but she also proved equal to the challenge, just as she always did.

Immediately Mary sprang into action. Her heart pounding with fear, she packed their few belongings and food for the trip. Then she and Joseph escaped with Jesus into the darkness, with only the stars to guide them. Remember, there is no reason to think that Joseph was an experienced international traveler either! Perhaps they traveled alone, or maybe they hooked up with some kind of caravan or group of merchants. But the family would have had to be circumspect and cautious about their identity, lest word get back to Herod. They were headed to a strange land, not knowing when or even if they would ever see their relatives again. Although by that time in history there was a Jewish community in Egypt, Mary probably wondered where they would live and how Joseph would find work.

The journey to Egypt took at least ten days. Much of it was downhill and across a desert of sand dunes, the same southern desert described in the Book of Exodus. The apocryphal gospels tell far-fetched stories that make the trip seem a cinch: palm trees bending to give dates to the family, robbers in awe and leaving the travelers alone upon seeing the child, lions and leopards adoring Jesus, the family magically arriving in Egypt in no time. In reality, the three refugees would have experienced the heat of the scorching desert sun, dirt, insects, hunger and fatigue and spent nights sleeping outside without shelter.

Mary's imagination was probably working overtime as the couple tried to distance themselves from the murderous king. In her mind's eye she must have pictured the Roman soldiers pursuing them. No doubt she glanced back often, straining her ears to listen for their horses' hoof beats.

Once again, Mary was not in control of her life and was faced with mystifying events. If it was true that her baby was the Son of God, then why were they being subjected to such trials? Why didn't God protect his own Son from harm? Mary had no answers but continued on in sheer faith. She would not be the last friend of God called to venture into threatening, uncharted territory on the journey of life.

Into and Out of Egypt (Matthew 2:13-23)

The Holy Family was successful in evading the Roman soldiers who, at King Herod's command, slaughtered all boys in and around Bethlehem who were two years old or younger. Scholars estimate that about thirty were killed. Word of the massacre of the innocent children probably trickled down to Egypt and horrified Mary. She must have held her baby even closer and thanked God for his safety.

In the Church of John the Baptist in Ain Karem is a cave where Elizabeth and Zechariah are presumed to have hidden their son John when the soldiers from Herod came to kill the baby boys.

Legends say that the Holy Family settled in a town a few miles northeast of today's city of Cairo. Visitors are shown a fountain from which Jesus supposedly made fresh waters spring. In Cairo there is also an old sycamore where presumably the travelers rested.

Some think that Matthew told the story of the flight into Egypt in order to parallel the life of Jesus with that of Moses. As a baby, that great Old Testament hero was spared while the pharaoh had other baby boys killed. Moses lived to lead his people out of slavery to new life in the Promised Land, which is precisely what Jesus did for all. Another possible motive for including the story was to fulfill the prophecy, "Out of Egypt I have called my son," which Matthew quotes. On the other hand, given King Herod's outrageous behavior in other matters, the flight into Egypt is very plausible as historical fact.

The Holy Family lived as immigrants in Egypt for perhaps a year or two. Then one night an angel came to Joseph in a dream again and instructed him to take his family back to Israel, because Herod was dead. Apparently Joseph had planned to settle in the southern region of Judea—perhaps in Bethlehem, the town of his ancestors. But in another dream he was warned that Herod's cruel son Archelaus ruled there. So the Holy Family went on further to Nazareth, which was certainly Mary's home town and became Jesus'. Matthew's Gospel remarks that this was to fulfill the prophecy, "He will be called a Nazorean." The long journey from Egypt back through the desert to Nazareth, carrying a young, perhaps still nursing child was another physical ordeal for Mary to endure.

Life in Nazareth

The Gospels are silent about the next years of Jesus' life, until he is about thirty, except for one event when he was twelve, which is described in the next chapter. Jesus spent this long period, "the hidden life of Jesus," living as a normal human being in a family and a neighborhood, creating a reservoir of experiences to draw on later when he became a wandering teacher and missionary.

During all these years, Mary was with the Son of God—face-to-face and day-in/day-out. He was her little boy. She played with him, kissed him, and ruffled his hair. They ate together, prayed together, laughed together, and no doubt cried together. Mary taught Jesus how eat, trained him in good manners, and imparted her values to him. Imagine the conversations they had!

Mary's vocation was to oversee the development of the God-man from conception to adulthood. As far as we know, only one vision—the original one when the angel appeared—sustained her in this work. Her greatness lies in her faith and fidelity.

We don't know how long Joseph lived. The scripture is silent on that question. If he were an older man when he married Mary, he might have died when Jesus was still a teenager or young adult. Or he might have died of one of the many diseases that killed people at an early age in those days. We do know that he was known as a carpenter by the people in the village and that Jesus too was referred to as "the carpenter, the son of Mary" (Mark 6:3). Joseph would have taught Jesus his carpenter trade, so that later Jesus could support his mother and himself. Perhaps when Jesus was old enough, he and Joseph would have occasionally left Mary for a few days to do construction work in Sepphoris, a nearby town that was being rebuilt by the Romans. Whatever the true story, we can assume that Jesus loved Joseph and vice versa, for when Jesus came to describe God, he used the analogy of "Father" to do so.

The Gospel of Luke sums up the "hidden" years in Nazareth by saying, "And Jesus grew and became strong, filled with wisdom, and the favor of God was upon him" (Luke 2:40). This means that Jesus did not emerge from the womb like some miniature adult but rather learned from Mary and Joseph. He couldn't have had two better teachers.

In all the unusual and stressful events that followed the Annunciation, Mary did what she had to do, with no fanfare and no hysterics. She acted with calm, quiet dignity and maturity beyond her years. God chose the right woman to carry out the extraordinary mission of bringing Jesus to the world and the world to Jesus.

Listening Mother
Finding a Lost Jesus

What mother hasn't had the harrowing experience of temporarily losing a child? While shopping, she suddenly finds that her toddler isn't at her side, or at the beach she can't see her preteen in the water, or one night her adolescent or young adult is especially late coming home. The minutes seem like hours until the child is found. And sometimes, of course, the child is not found, or is found hurt or even dead. Luke's Gospel is the only one to provide a story from the hidden life of Jesus. He tells how Jesus was missing—not for an hour or two but for three painfully long days that must have felt like three years to Mary.

The Passover Journey (Luke 2:41-50)

Mary and Joseph observed the Passover by traveling to Jerusalem each year they possibly could. The law required only men thirteen or older who lived within eighteen miles of Jerusalem to make the journey. The fact that both Joseph and Mary made this journey regularly, even though they lived about 100 miles away, shows how devout this couple was. When Jesus was twelve, he accompanied his parents for the days of the festival. Maybe it was the first time they allowed him to accompany them.

On the way home that year, Mary and Joseph presumed that their son was somewhere in the caravan. Because sometimes the women traveled separately from the men, Mary might have assumed Jesus was with Joseph and Joseph that Jesus was with her. Or they could have thought that he was with other boys his age. Even when the couple realized that Jesus was missing, they continued to travel for a day, looking for him among their rela-

*Let Mary teach us
how to treasure in our
hearts the mystery of
God who for our sake
became man; and may
she help us to bear
witness in our world to
His truth, His love, and
His peace.*

—Pope Benedict XVI

tives and friends who formed a straggling line wending its way back to Nazareth. No one had seen him. So Mary and Joseph turned around and retraced their steps to Jerusalem. All the way, they must have been thinking the worst, just as all parents do. Remember, this was a child that King Herod had already tried to have murdered.

In part, Mary's anxiety would have been caused by the thought that her boy must be desperately searching for them too. This did not prove to be the case. Back in Jerusalem, Mary and Joseph looked for Jesus everywhere—where they had stayed and where they had eaten the Passover meal. Frantic with worry, they searched the streets and knocked on doors with an increasing sense of urgency. We can imagine how heart-wrenching losing Jesus must have been for both Mary and Joseph. Not only was he their beloved and only son, but they knew that he was God's Son, entrusted to them for safekeeping.

Finally the couple went back to the Temple. They probably thought that this would be the last place they would find a child, but there Jesus was, sitting in the middle of the teachers, listening to them, asking and answering questions, and amazing them with his understanding and answers. Mary and Joseph didn't know what to think. Relief and anger most likely battled in their hearts. What Jesus had done seemed inconsiderate to say the least, dangerous in many ways, and incomprehensible to the simple rural people Joseph and Mary were.

Mary spoke first, not Joseph, and her words were typical of any mother whose adolescent has done something shocking. Her manner, however, was dignified. She didn't yell and scream and carry on, but before all the teachers Mary chided gently, "Child, why have you treated us like this? Look, your father and I have been searching for you in great anxiety." Notice how Mary, ever sensitive to Joseph's feelings, not merely her own, included her husband in her complaint. As head of the Holy Family, Joseph was also responsible for the well-being of the Son of God, and Mary acknowledged this.

Jesus replied, "Why were you searching for me? Did you not know that I must be in my Father's house?" These, Jesus' first words recorded in Scripture, are his first claim that God is his father. Neither Mary nor Joseph could make sense out of this perplexing response. Yes, the Temple was the house of God and Jesus was God's Son, but why would he take it upon himself to stay behind without telling them and engage in a discussion with a bunch of adults he didn't even know? "They did not understand what he said to them," says the Gospel.

This story makes us wonder what other words and actions of Jesus puzzled his parents as he grew up under their roof. Mary, certainly, would have many causes for wonder and heartache as she followed her son through his life and public ministry. As Luke records, "His mother treasured all these things in her heart" (Luke 2:51).

Years in Nazareth

The Gospel assures us that Jesus accompanied his parents home: "Then he went down with them and came to Nazareth, and was obedient to them" (Luke 2:51).

Losing Jesus for three days must have been traumatic for Mary, but it was just another test of her faith and one of the seven sorrows that Simeon predicted would pierce her heart. This loss foreshadowed two other sorrows that are not usually listed among the seven: the death of Joseph and Jesus leaving home to begin his public ministry.

fyi...

According to tradition, the Holy House of Loreto in Loreto, Italy, is the house of the Holy Family in Nazareth. It was miraculously carried there from Palestine by angels after temporary stays at two other sites. The cottage sits within an enormous basilica. Since at least the fifteenth century it has been a popular shrine. Recent popes have visited and prayed there. The Litany of Loreto (see pages 159-161) is named for this site. The transported house gave rise to Mary's being declared patroness of aviators and our praying to her for safe air flights.

Marian Monogram

A monogram for Mary combines all the letters in the name Maria:

We don't know when or how Joseph died, but the fact that he is not mentioned again in Scripture leads us to believe that he died sometime before Jesus began his public ministry. This would have been a great loss for both Mary and Jesus, since they were such a tight-knit family. Plus it would have put a lot of pressure on Jesus to remain in Nazareth to care for his mother, which he apparently did until he was about thirty years old.

On one hand, his finally leaving Nazareth must have been a relief for Mary, who patiently waited for Jesus to begin his public ministry. As year after year passed, she had probably been concerned about her adult son. Was he going to be a carpenter all his life? When was he going to begin his work of bringing about the good news of salvation? Moreover, Jesus was unmarried, which definitely set him apart from the other thirty-year-old men. Perhaps her concern for what people thought about her son mirrored her feelings about what they had thought about her when she got pregnant or even about her and Joseph having only one child.

On the other hand, after being so close to Jesus all those years, Mary must have felt acute sorrow in watching Jesus close up his carpentry shop. She must have cried the day she said good-bye to her only son. The weeks after he left, she would have felt the separation keenly. The house would seem empty, especially if she had no one to cook for besides herself. And like all mothers whose children leave the nest, Mary would always be wondering what her son was doing, if he was all right, and if he was eating well. In addition, Mary would now have to depend on the kindness of relatives and neighbors for companionship and help.

One day when Jesus, now on his own, was visiting his friends Martha, Mary and their brother Lazarus in Bethany, Martha bustled about preparing

for your spiritual health...

Mary is a model of reflecting on and treasuring God's words and actions. From time to time read a passage of Scripture about her and let your mind dwell on the words. Ponder what they mean for you and your life.

*The name of Mary is
the key of the gates of
heaven.*

—St. Ephrem

food while her sister Mary sat at his feet listening to him. These two sisters exemplify respectively the active and contemplative sides of Christian life. The Blessed Mother, also named Mary, beautifully combined both aspects: She actively ministered to her parents, to Elizabeth, to Jesus and Joseph and others; yet she sustained a vibrant interior life of union with God.

The "Martha" side of Mary came into play not only as Mary took care of her own family day after day but also as she practiced the works of mercy toward others. We can picture Mary at the well, exchanging smiles and kind words with the other women, taking flowers to a sick neighbor, inviting people over to share some warm, fresh bread, and giving advice to a younger woman in the village. Her "Mary" side was manifested as she gazed in wonder at her son, contemplated God's mysterious workings in her life, reflected on the words of Scripture, and watched the sunset over Nazareth with Joseph and Jesus. These are the simple things that made Mary holy. To her contemporaries, she was an ordinary person and so was her son, but we know better.

Mediatrix of All Graces
Intercession at a Wedding

The Gospel of John doesn't include many miracles, but it is the only one to narrate the story of the miracle at Cana. The author of this Gospel is a theologian and a poet whose writing has many undertones. This particular miracle at a wedding feast is charged with meaning. For one thing, John presents Mary in a role that is very familiar to us: that of intercessor. Although Scripture calls Jesus the one mediator, because he was the bridge between humankind and God, Mary supports and shares in this role. Her power is derived from Jesus' merits. She's the "mediatrix" to Jesus as mediator. In other words, when we call, "Mary," she calls, "Jesus," on our behalf.

Thousands of stories can be told about Mary's help. Sister Mary Maris Geiger, a member of my community, the Sisters of Notre Dame, recounts how as a young sister she contracted tuberculosis and was given one week to live. One day, confined to bed, coughing up blood, and too weak to hold a prayer book, she spoke to Mary in her heart saying, "Mary, I don't deserve to see you as Bernadette did, but if you want to, you can cure me." Immediately a light came into the room, moved along the side of the bed, stayed at the foot, and then moved back through the doorway. While the light was there, Sister felt her strength return. The doctor was amazed. In people who recover from tuberculosis, its germ remains incased in their lungs. Sister's x-rays showed no trace of it. In 1949, Sister Maris, one of her order's first missionaries, went to India, where she still ministers today in 2007.

The Wedding (John 2:1-11)

Cana is a town in Galilee. The Gospel says that Mary was at a wedding there, and then adds, almost as a footnote, that Jesus and his disciples had also been invited. Mary is singled out as the key figure here, not Jesus. Perhaps she played some role in planning the celebration. Undoubtedly, she and the other women cooked and served the food for the days of feasting.

During the party Mary noticed that the wine ran out, a crisis that would ruin the celebration. She stated the bare fact to her son, "They have no wine." Jesus replied somewhat coolly, "Woman, what concern is that to you and to me? My hour has not yet come." Still, Mary knew Jesus well enough to expect him to do something, although she didn't know exactly what. Because she believed

Mary, Star of the Sea

St. Jerome called Mary a drop (stillis) of the sea. By mistake, a copyist wrote "a star (stella)" of the sea. This name (Stella Maris) fit Mary as our heavenly spiritual guide. She became known under this title as the protectress of seafarers. St. Bernard of Clairvaux wrote a lovely reflection on this title: "Whoever you are, tossed about by the gales and storms of the ocean of life, fix your gaze on the 'Star of the Sea,' who is Mary. In dangers, in difficulties, in doubts, think of Mary and call on her to help you. Let her name be ever on your lips; let her love be ever in your heart. With her for a guide, you will never go astray. If you pray to her, you will never lose heart. If she bears you up, you will not fall. If she leads you, you will never weary. If she helps you, you will reach the harbor."

in Jesus already, she directed the servants, "Do whatever he tells you." It is interesting to note that these are the last words of Mary recorded in Scripture and sum up Mary's advice regarding her son. This has been called Mary's commandment.

Some theologians explain that the hour Jesus referred to was the hour of his death and resurrection, when his glory would be revealed to all people. Another interpretation is that the hour he meant was the hour he began his public ministry. If so, then this hour was advanced purely because of Mary's prayer. Because of her, he worked his first miracle and revealed himself to the public for the first time.

In addressing Mary as "woman," Jesus was not being rude. This was a title of respect and honor, which he used again in John's Gospel when he spoke to her from the cross, when his "hour" had truly come. The use of "woman" also makes us think of the prophecy in Genesis that foretold that the offspring of the woman would crush the serpent's head.

In any case, Jesus didn't disappoint his mother. There were six stone jars, each jar holding twenty to thirty gallons, that were used for purification rites. Jesus told the servants to fill them with water. The servants obeyed Mary and did what Jesus told them, even though it must have seemed inane to them. They were probably neighbors or relatives that Mary knew.

When the servants filled the jars to the brim, Jesus directed them to take some of the "water" to the chief steward. After tasting the wine, the steward called the bridegroom over and said, "Everyone serves the good wine first, and then the inferior wine after the guests have become drunk. But you have kept the good wine until now." Jesus had given the couple a fantastic wedding present.

After the wedding Jesus, Mary, his brothers, and

Holy Land site...

The actual site of Cana is undetermined. One possibility is the Cana frequented by tourists that is four miles from Nazareth. A Catholic church there displays an ancient large jar like the jars that held the water and then the wine in the miracle.

his disciples went to Capernaum and stayed there a few days. Jesus was now ready to begin his public ministry, which had just been jump-started by his own mom!

The Meaning behind the Miracle

The Cana miracle was the first one Jesus worked. It revealed his power and glory, and the Gospel states that it prompted his disciples to believe in him. Perhaps, being a good mother, Mary really involved her son in the wedding problem because she desired to encourage him to begin his work as Messiah. She saw the opportunity to give him the nudge he needed, and she grabbed it.

This miracle was a response to people's ordinary needs in the midst of daily life. This changing water into wine to spare the groom embarrassment has been called "the kind miracle." Kindness was one of the virtues that his mother had cultivated in Jesus. Mary's solicitude for the newlyweds and their families is another example of how Mary's holiness was demonstrated by doing good in little ways—something every one of us can do.

Wine is associated with joy and celebration. Making wine from water is a sign that the new creation is beginning. It heralds the hour when Jesus will save us and usher in a new heaven and new earth. This miracle of changing water into wine also foreshadows the Eucharist, when Jesus changes wine into his blood, the blood that was shed for the salvation of the world.

This miracle at Cana is also a sign of God's lavish love. The wine Jesus provided was abundant—at least 130 gallons, more than enough for the guests, who already had drunk quite a bit. Jesus' wine was also excellent, proving that God is extravagant in his care for people.

Our Lady of the Cape

A new church was to be built for Cap-de-la-Madeleine on the shore of the St. Lawrence River in Quebec, Canada. In 1879, the stone was to be hauled across the mile-wide river after it had frozen. That winter, however, was so mild that the river had open water and only a thin sheet of ice. The pastor, Father Desilets, prayed to Mary on March 14, promising that if an ice-bridge formed across the river he would not destroy the former church, a chapel that had been dedicated to her in 1662. In three days the river miraculously became solid ice, strong enough to hold more than 150 horse-drawn sledges hauling the huge stone across.

True to his promise, Fr. Desilets renovated the old chapel. On the evening of the day he consecrated it to Mary in 1888, he, a young priest, and a lame man prayed before the statue of Mary. It showed Mary with a white veil, standing on a globe, and crushing a serpent. On her chest was a large gold flaming heart circled by roses. All three men saw the statue's downcast eyes open and gaze above their heads. The statue was crowned, and a rosary with wood from Gethsemane's olive trees was placed on her arm. Today Our Lady of the Cape is the national shrine of Canada.

The miracle at the Cana wedding is also viewed as God's bestowing a blessing on marriages. It is the scriptural basis for the sacrament of matrimony, through which God gives a couple the graces they need to love each other exclusively and forever and to be open to bringing children into the world.

Mary as Go-Between

From Jesus' reaction to his mother's suggestion, it

seems that he wasn't quite ready to go public and declare himself as the Messiah. Yet because Mary was counting on him, he changed his plans and supplied the wine, showing that he is a good son who responds to the wishes of his mother. This is the reason why we Catholics pray to Mary for certain favors and graces and give her grand titles such as Mediatrix of All Graces and Omnipotent Suppliant. We look to Mary to intercede for us, and she does, not only because she is our mother but also because—as a member of the Communion of Saints (the Church on earth, in heaven, and in purgatory)—she is bound to us. In the plan of salvation, Church members experience solidarity. We are united as mediators for one another, praying for one another privately and also communally, such as in the general intercessions at Mass. Notice too that when we pray the Our Father and the Hail Mary, we pray not just for ourselves but for all of us: "forgive *our* trespasses," "*our* daily bread," "*us* sinners," and "*our* death."

Just as we are supported and gain strength from the prayers of our friends and relatives on earth, we are still helped by them after they die. Scripture urges us on in the race to heaven "since we are surrounded by so great a cloud of witnesses" (Hebrews 12:1). The saints in heaven are with us; they are merely on a new level of existence. Certainly Mary, the holiest member of the Communion of Saints, can pray for us too. She is our most powerful prayer partner and advocate.

When you wanted something from your father, did you ever ask your mother to speak to him for you? Did it work? Approaching Mary to act on our behalf is similar. However, we should not set her in contrast to God and see God as the strict, just father and Mary as the gentle, merciful mother. Mary's love for us helps us appreciate God's love. In fact,

God explains his love for us this way: "Can a woman forget her nursing child, or show no compassion for the child of her womb? Even these may forget, yet I will not forget you. See, I have inscribed you on the palms of my hands" (Isaiah 49:15–16).

Perfect Disciple
Jesus' Preaching

During the thirty years that Jesus lived with Mary, they must have had innumerable conversations about God and the kingdom that Jesus was about to inaugurate. Then when Jesus left home and began preaching in Galilee, it's likely that Mary occasionally joined the crowd listening to him, although like any good mother she would have stayed in the background.

Return to Nazareth

One day, Jesus returned to Nazareth and preached brilliantly in its synagogue there. Chances are that Mary sat in the women's gallery. She would have proudly witnessed their neighbors' awe at her son's wisdom. She would have been saddened terribly, however, when their admiration turned to skepticism and then outright rage because Jesus performed only a few cures for his fellow Nazoreans. He said he was amazed by their "lack of faith" (Mark 6:1-6).

Imagine the pain and horror in Mary's heart when the mob chased her son out of the synagogue, drove him out of town, and attempted to throw him off a cliff. Imagine too the awkwardness and humiliation Mary endured ever afterwards, when she had to live and interact with those same people, who were her neighbors.

Later, word would reach Mary that her son was accused of being a glutton and a drunkard. Moreover, he was causing scandal by breaking the Sabbath to heal people. How this news had to upset her and made her dread what lay ahead for her son. Simeon's dire prophecy must have hung heavy in her heart.

In Nazareth is the Convent of Our Lady of Fear, the traditional site where Mary shook with fear when the villagers pursued Jesus. Not far from this is a hill with a steep cliff known as "Leap of the Lord" hill.

Tension with the Family

Jesus' behavior caused tension in the family. One sad line in Scripture states, "Not even his brothers believed in him" (John 7:5). The Gospel of Mark, the earliest gospel, recounts that when people took offense at him in Nazareth, Jesus replied, "Prophets are not without honor, except in their hometown, and among their own kin, and in their own house" (Mark 6:4). This implies that even Mary might have had a difficult time understanding her son's behavior. It was no easy mission to be the mother of the Messiah—especially a rejected Messiah.

Once after preaching and healing, Jesus went home again, and so many people followed that he and the apostles couldn't even eat. When his family heard that people were saying that he was out of his mind or—worse—possessed by Satan, a delegation of his family members came to talk sense into him. Was Mary part of this delegation? We don't know, but we can certainly surmise Mary would never have lost faith in Jesus, no matter how worried she might have been about him.

There are two times when Jesus seemed to distance himself from his family and in particular his mother. One day while he was preaching, Mary and Jesus' brothers tried to reach him, but the crowd was too large. When the word came to Jesus that his family was there to see him, he replied, "My mother and my brothers are those who hear the word of God and do it" (Luke 8:21). Later a similar scene occurred. A woman in the crowd exclaimed to Jesus, "Blessed is the womb that bore you and the breasts that nursed you!" This reference to Mary echoes Elizabeth's, "Blessed are you among women," and fulfills Mary's Magnificat prophecy, "All generations will call me blessed." But Jesus contradicted the woman, saying, "Blessed rather are those who hear

Our Lady of Prompt Succor

The people of New Orleans turn to Our Lady of Prompt Succor, the patroness of their city, in times of trial. Mother St. Michel Gensoul, an Ursuline sister in France, wanted to teach in New Orleans. When her bishop refused to let her go, she petitioned the pope and prayed to Mary, promising that if the pope answered yes, she would promote devotion to Mary under the title of Our Lady of Prompt Succor. The pope gave permission, so Sr. Gensoul commissioned a statue of Mary holding the infant Jesus, and in 1810 she took it to New Orleans with her. Two years later, a great fire threatened the convent. After the statue was brought to the window and Sister Gensoul prayed, wind changed the fire's direction.

During Hurricane Katrina in August of 2005, the shrine where the statue is housed had extensive roof damage. However, on the following January 8, the Feast of Our Lady of Prompt Succor, the 192nd annual Mass of Thanksgiving was celebrated there. One hurricane victim quipped that Our Lady must have been away from her desk on August 29!

quick quote...

His mother is the entire Church, because by God's grace, she brings forth the members of Jesus Christ, that is to say, those who are faithful to him.

—St. Augustine

the word of God and obey it" (Luke 11:27–28).

Both of these responses of Jesus sound like putdowns of his family and especially his mother. How could Jesus have snubbed her, and in public at that? We hope that she realized as we do that it is Mary who fits Jesus' description of the perfect disciple. Mary lived her entire life listening to God and doing his will. According to St. Augustine it was a greater honor for Mary to have been Jesus' disciple than to have been his mother. In these often-misunderstood passages from Luke, Jesus was not canceling his praise for his mother but rather shifting his reason for it. This is good news for us, for while

From time to time ex-
amine your life. Are
you following the ex-
ample of Mary: hear-
ing the Word of God
and then doing it?

none of us can be Jesus' mother we can all share in her role as disciple.

All disciples can look to Mary, our sister in the faith, as a model of what it means to follow Jesus. Mary gave herself to a radical, total living of the gospel. She was ever open to God's plans and did her best to fulfill them, no matter what it cost her. Despite doubt, confusion, uncertainty and pain, Mary remained faithful. Her love for God was unmatched.

When it becomes difficult to live the gospel, when being a Christian invites scorn or causes conflict with others or within ourselves, Mary can be our inspiration. If we pattern ourselves on her and hold fast to the Word of God, we too will be blessed family members of Jesus. Micah 6:8 expresses in a nutshell what God calls us to do to be holy: "to do justice, and to love kindness, and to walk humbly with your God." Mary is the incarnation of these words. She points the way to the kingdom of God— on earth as it is in heaven.

Sorrowful Mother
The Execution of Jesus

The image of any mother watching her child die is heartrending. John's Gospel present us with a horrifying scene: Jesus suspended on a rough wood cross by nails pounded through his hands and feet, drenched in his own blood, a circlet of thorns on his head. Standing at the foot of the cross, watching all this, is Mary, his mother. The intense sorrow Mary, the gentlest and most sensitive of persons, endured has led the Church to apply to her the words of the Book of Lamentations: "Is it nothing to you, all you who pass by? Look and see if there is any sorrow like my sorrow" (Lamentations 1:12).

The Way of the Cross

It would have been easier for Mary to stay out of sight and wait for news of her son's fate at the hands of the Roman and Jewish authorities. This was what most of his closest followers did, except for John, Mary Magdalene, and a few other women. Mary, however, was made of sterner stuff. Her love and loyalty impelled her to be with her son, even if things were going to end badly. She must have wondered at the time what had happened to the promises that had been proclaimed by the angels and shepherds and magi.

Mary participated in the passion of Jesus from beginning to end. Since we know she was in Jerusalem on Friday, it is very possible—likely even— that she was present at the Last Supper the night before. The Scriptures don't say. One reason people think there were only twelve men at the Last Supper is because of the famous painting by Leonardo da Vinci, which played such an important role in the popular fictional book and movie *The*

One tradition that
arose in Rome is that
Mary fainted when
she saw Jesus carry-
ing his cross. This is
commemorated by a
non-traditional station
of the cross, called
"the Spasm of Mary,"
but this belief is not
fostered by the
Church, which stress-
es Mary's inner
strength.

Inside the Basilica of
the Holy Sepulcher is
a hill thought to be
Calvary. Near the hill
is a shrine with the
image of the Sorrow-
ful Mother.

Da Vinci Code.

In any case, as soon as Mary received word on
Thursday night that Jesus had been taken prisoner,
she must have tried to go to him. When Pilate asked
if, as a Passover favor, the people wished him to release the rebel Barabbas or Jesus, perhaps Mary was
in the crowd. If so, for a moment she might have
had a glimmer of hope. Then her heart sank when
the mob chose to free Barabbas and Pilate ordered
Jesus to be scourged. Her heart ached not only for
her son but also for her people, who were rejecting
their Messiah. A while later, after the vicious whip-
ping, Mary might have witnessed Pilate presenting
her son, bruised and bleeding. She would have
heard the mob shout, "Crucify him. Crucify him."
The images of Mary in the Mel Gibson movie *The
Passion of the Christ,* especially her observing the
torturing of Jesus and then cleaning up the blood of
her son afterward, are too painful for a lot of people
to watch.

It is customary to sing verses of the *"Stabat Mater
Dolorosa"* (first line, "At the cross her station keeping") while praying the Stations of the Cross. (See
pages 166-169 for the complete words.) According
to tradition, Mary followed Jesus as he struggled to
carry the heavy beam of his cross to Calvary, his
blood staining the ground. She saw him fall on the
rough, narrow street as he made his way through
the jeering people. She saw him manhandled by
the Roman soldiers. When Simon was recruited to
help bear the wood, Mary must have been grateful
to him. How she wished that she herself could ease
her son's pain.

The fourth station of the Stations of the Cross is
"Jesus Meets His Mother." We can imagine the sorrowful, yet loving, communication that occurred at
that meeting. Perhaps it was silent, conveyed only
through eyes. Certainly part of the agony Jesus suf-

fered was knowing that his torture was causing his mother such extreme pain. On the other hand, her presence would have comforted him like none other. She was one with him in his redemptive mission, selflessly accomplishing what needed to be done for the salvation of the world.

Gift from the Cross

On Calvary, Mary stood looking on as her son was stripped and the angry red wounds on his body revealed. Then she heard the nails pounded through Jesus' hands and feet. She watched as the cross with his body suspended from it was hoisted up and set in place. She saw the Roman soldiers divide up Jesus' clothes and throw dice to see who would get the seamless tunic. It could be that Mary had woven these clothes herself for Jesus. She was not allowed to keep and treasure them in memory of her son.

Looking down from the cross, Jesus saw Mary and the beloved disciple standing next to her. The Church has understood this to be the apostle and evangelist St. John, although the Scriptures don't state this explicitly. After he died, Mary would be alone in the world, so Jesus arranged for her future, He said to his mother, "Woman, here is your son" (John 19:26) and to John, "Here is your mother" (John 19:27). John, Jesus' friend, would take Mary into his home and care for her as a son.

Since the time of St. Gregory of Tours, who lived in the sixth century, the Church has viewed the beloved disciple as our representative and believes that Jesus gave Mary to all of us as a mother, ratifying on Calvary the maternity she assumed at the Annunciation. Mary gave Jesus to us, and Jesus gave her to us. Mary is our precious legacy, a gift. She adopted us, taking us into her heart and loving us

fyi...

Devotion to the Sorrowful Mother (Mater Dolorosa), which arose in the late eleventh century, flourished during the Black Plague in the fourteenth century, when people needed consolation. The feast of the Mother of Sorrows is on September 15.

trivial tidbit...

A *pietà* is a representation of Mary holding the dead body of her son. The most famous is Michelangelo's statue in St. Peter's Basilica in Rome, which shows Mary with a young face. It is one of four *pietàs* he created.

big book search...

Read John's story of Jesus' death in John 19:16–42.

as she loved her firstborn son. We, in turn, love and honor her. Mary is concerned for our welfare and eager to pray to her son, our brother, for us. Daily we look to our heavenly mother for help as we pray the Hail Mary or speak to her in our own words.

The End

For three excruciating hours Mary stood there helplessly while her beloved son suffered and people—even the criminals crucified on either side—scoffed at him. She heard Jesus say, "Father, forgive them; for they do not know what they are doing" (Luke 23:34) and "I am thirsty" (John 19:28). In desolation herself, she identified with him as he called out, "My God, my God, why have you forsaken me?" (Mark 15:34) She was moved and heartened when Jesus said to the good thief, "Truly I tell you, today you will be with me in Paradise" (Luke 23:43). Finally she heard Jesus' loud cry, "Father, into your hands I commend my spirit," (Luke 23:46) and his last words, "It is finished." Mary, who had seen Jesus take his first breath in Bethlehem, watched him draw his final breath on Calvary. His sacrifice was completed.

Then she witnessed a Roman soldier thrust a lance into Jesus' chest to make sure he was dead. Mary must have gasped and felt the lance enter her heart too. Water and blood flowed out from the side of Jesus. This event is identified as the birth of his Church. And Mary was there, just as she had been at the birth of Jesus, some thirty-odd years earlier. She must have drawn some comfort from a centurion's pronouncement, "Truly this man was God's Son" (John 15:39).

The crowds dispersed, but Mary along with the Galilean women and acquaintances stayed. In the evening she was probably there to see Joseph of Arimathea and Nicodemus lower the body of Jesus from the cross. A flood of memories must have washed over Mary—the day she first wrapped him in swaddling clothes, presents he had given her, finding him in the Temple, the wedding at Cana. Joseph and Nicodemus wrapped the corpse in linen and placed it in a new tomb carved out of rock. Mary watched them bury her son. Now a childless widow, she went home with the beloved disciple.

Mary's long vigil was over. For this, her son had come into the world—to be its Redeemer. And she was the one of the few who had the stamina, the courage, and the love to see his sacrifice through to the end. United to Jesus, she offered him to the Father.

Surely Mary's faith was tested on Calvary as she shared the darkness and abandonment of her son's destiny. Not only her son had died, but her Messiah as well. We do not know how well Mary understood God's plan for our redemption. Maybe she didn't know that the tragic, shameful death would ultimately lead to the triumph of the empty tomb. If so, this was a time of confusion and insecurity for Mary. Yet, her faith was unshakeable. Like Jesus, she accepted the cup God presented and trusted that all would work out for the good. In obedience, faith and love, Mary echoed the *"Fiat"* ("Let it be") she originally said at the Annunciation.

The experience of the cross earned for Mary the titles Mother of Sorrows and Queen of Martyrs. A martyr—the word means "witness"— is someone who died for the faith. Jesus was the first martyr. Mary was a martyr not in body but in spirit. Simeon's predictions that had haunted her life all came to pass. Jesus' passion was her passion. She shared in his agony as only a mother could. The cross she took up and carried was the mental anguish of watching her flesh and blood be hated, tortured

a cool website...

The National Sanctuary of Our Sorrowful Mother is in Portland Oregon. See www.thegrotto.org. A film of the beautiful Stations of the Cross being made by a group of pilgrims at the grotto is available on DVD at www. actapublications.com.

trivial tidbit...

Hispanics call Holy Saturday "the Solitude of Mary," when she waited in faith and hope for her son.

and killed. In essence, these sufferings were the birth pangs of her spiritual motherhood. Her sacrifice brought us new life.

The exquisite psychological pain Mary suffered prepared her to understand the pains we endure. Acquainted with sorrow, she is sympathetic to us who are still undergoing the trials of life on earth. She feels our pain and has compassion for us. With trust we can turn to her for help as we carry our own personal crosses. We know that Mary will stand with us by our cross.

Mother of the Church
Coming of the Holy Spirit

Scripture doesn't say a word about Jesus appearing to his mother after he rose from the dead. We can safely assume, however, that the two were reunited privately in a very intimate and touching meeting. How could that have not happened? Mary was not only Jesus' mother, she was his #1 disciple. We can only imagine the intense joy the mother and son shared and what they said to each other. In all probability, Mary was with the apostles Easter night when Jesus appeared to them. During the forty days before the Ascension, Jesus may have visited his mother other times too—either by herself or with others.

Then when Jesus left earth to return to heaven, Mary had to endure another leave-taking. Again, we can assume that Mary was present at the Ascension. This must have been a very different leave-taking from the one on Golgotha. Even though Jesus was leaving her again, this time it was in glory, and Mary would have realized that she would see her son again soon.

Mother to the Young Church

Scripture first presents Mary at the Annunciation, when she was overshadowed by the Holy Spirit and Jesus took form in her. The last glimpse of Mary that Scripture offers is at Pentecost, when the same Holy Spirit comes down upon her and the apostles, giving birth to the Church—the Body of Christ—as an institution. Thus, Mary is the only disciple who was present for the whole span of Jesus' life, from conception to childhood to public ministry to passion and death to resurrection to ascension and, finally, to Pentecost.

A charming legend highlights Mary's heart for sinners. One day Jesus asked St. Peter, the gatekeeper of heaven, why certain sinners were walking around paradise when he had banned them. Peter replied, "I shut the door to keep them out, but Mary opened the windows."

Mary in the Liturgy

Mary is mentioned at Mass when her son's sacrifice is celebrated on our altars—not only in the Nicene Creed but also in all four main Eucharistic Prayers and the seven alternate ones. Just as the Holy Spirit brought about the flesh and blood of Jesus in Mary, through the power of the same Spirit bread and wine become his body and blood at the Eucharist. At every liturgy we are joined by Mary and all the saints and angels in praising and thanking God. They are invisible but nonetheless present worshippers, joining us in what Catholics call the "Communion of Saints."

When Jesus ascended to heaven, he instructed the apostles to wait in Jerusalem for the Holy Spirit. They, along with Mary and other followers, stayed in an upstairs room and prayed. Other than the apostles, out of the 120 believers there, Mary is the only one Scripture names, highlighting the importance of her presence.

It must have been uncomfortable for the apostles to be with Mary after they had deserted her son in his hour of need. Peter had even denied knowing him. Mary's compassion and gentleness no doubt smoothed over the delicate situation and allayed their guilt and shame. After nine days, on the Jewish feast of Pentecost, a violent wind whooshed through the house. Tongues of fire appeared and settled on those gathered in the upper room, one on each. They were all filled with the Holy Spirit, who inspired them to speak in tongues, a supernatural gift of speaking a language that every foreigner in town could understand. From the inception of the Church, therefore, Mary was there, right in its midst, rapt in wonder at the miraculous events. Artists who recreate the Pentecost scene—like the

16th-century Spanish painter El Greco—set Mary, the Queen of Apostles, as the central figure.

Possibly Mary too received the gift of tongues, although Scripture is ambiguous. Mary's special gift, however, was to carry out her role as Mother of the Church. In the words of St. Augustine: "Mary is certainly the mother of the members of the Body of Christ, that is to say, our mother, because in her charity she cooperated in bringing forth in the Church the faithful who are the members of this divine head, whose mother she truly is according to the flesh."

Living with St. John, the beloved disciple, Mary probably guided the first members of the infant Church: answering their questions, giving advice, and telling them stories about her son. She would meet with them for the breaking of the bread, as the Eucharist was called. Just as Jesus had directed, she would eat the bread and drink the wine in memory of him, thereby receiving the same body and blood that she herself had given him at birth. Imagine that!

Just as Mary oversaw the initial growth of Jesus, who is the Head of the Church, so she was there for its first members. At first the Jewish Christians did not see themselves as a separate religion. Like the rest of them, Mary continued to go to the Temple, yet she now believed and understood that the Messiah who had been awaited for so long had truly come. And when the deacon Stephen was the first of many to be martyred and persecutions of the small group of followers of Jesus came, Mary suffered and grieved with the other believers. She must have been especially terrified of the man named Saul of Tarsus, who was leading the persecution, and all the more gratified when he finally encountered her son on the road to Damascus and became Paul, one of his most ardent and effective apostles.

fyi...

In September, 2006, Pope Benedict XVI visited the shrine of Our Lady of Altoetting, the most famous shrine of Our Lady in Germany. There is a statue of the Black Virgin there that dates back to 1330. In the chapel is a silver urn with the hearts of all the Bavarian kings. The Holy Father first prostrated himself before the Blessed Virgin and then donated his cardinal's ring to the poor on behalf of Mary.

Mother Through the Centuries

In Sweden's Lutheran
Cathedral of Västerås,
a fresh rose is always
kept on the altar of
the Blessed Virgin.

Beginning in the thirteenth century, some art depicts Mary as the Mother of Mercy, who wears a voluminous mantle under which she shelters small figures of members of the Church. Mary has also lived out her title of Mary, Help of Christians over and over in the course of history.

At first Mary was a living, breathing reality in the Church—the first among the disciples. After her life on earth ended, however, the Christians began to reflect on her role in salvation history. The earliest Marian prayer we have, which is from the third century, appeals to her to "hear our petitions." For two thousand years, people have turned to Mary for help, counting on her motherly love for them. They have written and uttered and sung countless beautiful prayers and hymns to her, invoking her aid. And she has always answered them, in one way or another.

During the Middle Ages, lives of Mary were written that included far-fetched stories emphasizing her maternal care for people. One story was about a nun who leaves the convent and marries. When she returns, she finds that Mary has taken her place so that she wouldn't be missed. In another story, when a criminal is being executed by hanging, Mary holds him up so that he doesn't die. When he is cut down, he runs away free.

Mary Today

Mary is still here for the Church. In fact, at the Second Vatican Council, Pope Paul VI gave her the official title Mother of the Church. This means that we as a Church as well as personally are never without our heavenly mother. In some cultures Mary is addressed familiarly as "mamma."

St. Maximilian Kolbe

The Franciscan priest Maximilian Mary Kolbe, who lived in Poland from 1894 to 1941, spread devotion to Mary Immaculate though the radio and literature, such as his monthly magazine entitled *The Knights of the Immaculate*. His pockets were usually filled with Miraculous Medals. (See description of this devotion on page 138.) He began an institute called the *Militia Immaculae* and founded spiritual centers called City of Mary. When the atomic bomb fell in Nagasaki, the City of Mary in that city was unharmed. During World War II, Fr. Kolbe was captured and sent to the concentration camp at Auschwitz. When ten men were to be starved to death as punishment for one who escaped, Fr. Kolbe voluntarily took the place of a man who had a family. According to Maximilian's mother, at the age of ten he had a vision of Mary offering him two crowns, the white crown of purity and the red crown of martyrdom. Mary asked which one he wanted, and he answered, "Both."

a cool website...

Cheri Lomonte has compiled a beautiful book titled *The Healing Touch of Mary: Real Life Stories from Those Touched by Mary.* Learn more or read or hear excerpts from the book at www.divineimpressions.com.

As our heavenly mother, Mary looks on us with maternal instincts. She is concerned about our well-being and has dreams and ambitions for us. The main one is that her son's sacrifice will not be in vain and that we will help carry out his mission on earth and join them in heaven when we have finished our time here.

Mary is a powerful ally in the face of temptations of every kind. She, whose image often shows her crushing the serpent, can secure grace for us to withstand the attacks and tricks of evil. St. John of Avila claimed, "If you are devoted to her, you will feel temptations melting away like wax before the fire."

fyi...

Our Lady of the Pillar is based on a legend that the apostle James, while preaching in Spain, saw Mary on a pillar carried by angels. The pillar is said to be the one venerated today in Zaragoz, Spain, where miracles of healings have been reported.

When we are in trouble because of sin, Mary prays for us. She, who is called Refuge of Sinners, is the personification of God's mercy. Gerard Manley Hopkins, S.J., in his poem "The Blessed Virgin Compared to the Air We Breathe" says: "We are wound/ with mercy round and round as if with air;" and then he names the air "Mary," who "mantles the guilty globe." The Church has always turned and will always turn to Mary as one who can channel God's mercy and grace to those in need.

Not only does Mary nurture the Church, but she is also the ideal member of the Church. As such, she is a model and teacher—which are both roles of every mother. We look to Mary to see what it means to be Christian, a person who loves, and we try to imitate her virtues. Mary is our touchstone for wholehearted commitment to God's will that is most perfectly manifested in our love for others. We pray that we may have a heart for others like the compassionate heart beating within Mary.

Mary is one with the Church. When the Second Vatican Council deliberated over whether or not to publish a separate document on Mary, the bishops decided to put her right where she belongs—in the document on the Church *(Lumen Gentium)*. Its last chapter is called "The Role of the Blessed Virgin Mary in the Mystery of Christ and the Church." In this chapter Mary is acknowledged as not only the Mother of God but also the mother of the whole human race. Her mission now is to help form Jesus within each one of us so that we all become other Christs.

Bridge to Unity

In the past, Mary was sometimes a source of contention between Catholics and Protestants. Today different Christian faith traditions are dialoguing about what they believe about Mary and arriving at a common understanding of her. For example, in 2002 a document called "Mary: Grace and Hope in Christ" was written jointly by Catholics and Anglicans. It is the result of drawing on the Scriptures and the common Christian tradition that predates the Reformation.

More and more Protestants are reclaiming Mary. Scot McKnight, an evangelical religious studies professor, colorfully explained it: "There are a few of us who are in a Trojan horse. It's as if we've been released in the Vatican, and we're swiping Mary and taking her back to the Protestant world."

Muslims, who regard Jesus as a great prophet, also highly esteem his mother Mary as a pure and holy saint. They, too, call her Our Lady, and the Qur'an upholds the Immaculate Conception and the virgin birth. Mary is the only woman named in the Qur'an. It has forty-two verses about her, more than the Bible. Chapter nineteen of the Qur'an is even titled "Mary." Perhaps Mary someday might provide a bridge for dialogue between Muslims and Christians.

short prayer...

My Mother, I put my trust in you.

Queen of Heaven
Mary's Crossing Over

A strong tradition exists that Mary spent the rest of her life in the care of St. John, the beloved disciple, in Ephesus. Originally a port city in Turkey, Ephesus became a center of Christianity, and the Ephesians received at least one letter from St. Paul, which is in the Bible. Ephesus was also the site of the Council that declared Mary to be the Mother of God. Interestingly, Ephesus had once been the city of the virgin goddess Artemis (Diana).

Today on the top of Nightingale Hill near Ephesus there is a shrine to Mary: A fourth-century church is combined with a two-story stone house of Roman architecture that is believed to be where Mary and John lived.

Mary's Assumption

We do not know how long Mary lived. Some scholars believe that she died in 48 A.D. In the past, some people prayed rosaries with 63 beads, one for each year of Our Lady's life. Regardless how long Mary lived after Jesus' death, surely she missed her son and husband every day and yearned to be reunited with them. Did Mary die? A few think that Mary was exempt from this punishment for sin. Most theologians, however, think that Mary underwent death—just as her son did and just as we all will do. The Eastern Church calls the passing of Mary the "dormition" or sleeping away.

There is an apocryphal book composed about 500 A.D. called *The Gospel of the Passing Away of Mary* or the *Pseudo-Melito,* because its author assumes the name of Melito, the second-century bishop of Sardis. It relates that when Mary is living again in her parents' house in Jerusalem and longing

England was given the title "Our Lady's Dowry" by St. Edward. A dowry is a gift of parents to a new couple. The title indicated that England was consecrated, given as a gift, to Mary. In 1061 St. Edward established England's national shrine of Our Lady of Walsingham as a new Nazareth, and it became one of the four most popular pilgrim sites of the Middle Ages. King Henry VIII destroyed the church and its statue of Mary, but in 1934 the National Shrine of Our Lady in Walsingham was re-inaugurated, and in 1954 Mary's statue there was crowned.

to see her son, an angel comes and foretells that she would be transported to heaven in three days. Mary asks that the apostles be present with her when this happens. Miraculously they are brought to her and so are present at her death. When they bury her, Jesus appears and has his angels take her body to paradise. An Arabic book adds that the chronically-late Thomas was missing and does not believe Mary had died. When the other apostles take him to her tomb and open it, they find it empty. In another version it is filled with roses and lilies.

The Roman Catholic Church has no formal teaching about Mary's death, one way or the other. What it does believe is that when Mary's life on earth was ended—whether she was in Jerusalem or Ephesus or somewhere else—she was immediately taken body and soul into heaven. In this way, God preserved her body from corruption—that body which had served his Son so well. This popular belief, called the Assumption, was declared a doctrine of faith in 1950, although the Church has believed it since the early centuries. One of the significances of the timing of this declaration is that it came right after World War II and the Holocaust, when the value of the human body was held in such low esteem. By insisting that Mary's body had been assumed into heaven, the Church was saying that the human body is sacred and important to God. The feast of the Assumption is celebrated on August 15 and for many years has been a holy day of obligation in the United States.

It is a point of fact that the remains of several other saints—such as St. John Vianney, St. Bernadette of Lourdes, and St. Catherine Labouré were discovered to be incorrupt, but these bodies are still on earth. There are no mortal remains of Mary, and the Church does not expect to find any. In Mary's case, there were no "first-class" relics, that

The Joys of Mary

Devotion to the joys of Mary actually predates devotion to her sorrows. They are first found in twelfth-century *Gaudes* (Rejoice)—Latin praises that tell Mary to rejoice because of five ways God has favored her. In the early fifteenth century, St. Bernardine of Siena and other Franciscans began promoting devotion to the following seven joys:

1. The Annunciation to the Blessed Virgin and the Incarnation of Our Lord (Luke 1:26-33, 38)
2. The Visitation of the Blessed Virgin to St. Elizabeth (Luke 1:39-45)
3. The Birth of Our Lord (Luke 2:6-12)
4. The Adoration of the Magi (Matthew 2:1-2, 10-11)
5. The Child Jesus Found in the Temple (Luke 2:41-50)
6. Resurrection of Our Lord (Mark 16:1-7)
7. Assumption of the Blessed Virgin into Heaven and Coronation as Queen of Heaven (Luke 1:46-55)

is, pieces of bone or hair, although some Eastern churches claim to have her mantle, her sash, her veil, and the like.

So, unlike the rest of us, Mary didn't have to wait until the end of the world for her body to be glorified and reunited with her soul. Right now she is already with her son in body and soul in heaven, worshipping God and enjoying eternal bliss. Having her body glorified makes Mary even more like Jesus. In this state, Mary is a sign and a promise of what awaits us. How Mary is now, God intends everyone to be someday. This truth gives us hope and consolation as we struggle with the trials, crises, sickness and death of physical life on earth.

Holy Land site...

In Jerusalem is the Church of the Tomb of the Virgin Mary built by the crusaders. Inside are altars dedicated to Joachim and Anne. On the lower level is the crypt of the traditional place of Mary's burial. In it is a tomb on which lies an effigy of Mary.

big book search...

Read Revelation 12:1-17 to learn more about the woman and the dragon.

quick quote...

St. John of Damascus said that as Mary enters heaven, the Temple of God, "David, her ancestor and God's relative, dances for joy (2 Sam 7:14); the angels dance in unison, the archangels applaud, and the powers of the heavens sing her glory."

In this one woman, who is the mother of us all, the ultimate destiny of the human race has already been realized. A helpful analogy is that we humans are like a fleet of ships in a storm at sea, and Mary is the first ship to reach the safe harbor.

Mary as Prototype of the Church

Certain people, objects and events in the Old Testament prefigure the New Testament. They anticipate what will happen. For example, the Exodus when God saved the Hebrews from slavery in Egypt and led them to the Promised Land, prefigured Jesus saving the human race from sin and leading us to heaven.

Mary prefigures, or is a type of, the Church in several ways so that Pope John Paul II in the encyclical *Mother of the Redeemer* can state that the Church "proceeds along the path already trodden by the Virgin Mary." Just as Mary brought forth Christ, so does the Church—sometimes called Mother Church—bring him into the world. Just as Mary was preserved from sin, so was the Church cleansed from all sin by the saving power of Jesus. Just as Mary was assumed into heaven, so will the Church be at the end of the world. Mary is the first flowering of the Church. In the words of theologian Karl Rahner, "God's grace is doing in us what he did in her."

Mary's Queenship

Today, when there aren't too many queens in the world, we may be more comfortable with looking on Mary as a companion. A purely human being, a creature like us, Mary is not beyond us but with us on our journey of faith. Her journey is completed, and now she prays with us and for us. Especially in times of need, Mary is present to support us. In short, she is not frozen in time, but a living reality.

However, Queen is the final image Scripture gives us of Mary. The last book of the Bible, the Book of Revelation, is a style of writing called "apocalyptic," which is meant to encourage those who are being persecuted for the faith. In this book there is a symbolic story of a struggle between a woman and a dragon. The woman is clothed with the sun, with the moon at her feet and a crown of twelve stars on her head. She gives birth to a son, the ruler of all nations, whom the dragon tries to devour. The woman has been interpreted to stand for Israel and also for the Church. Later the Church saw this queen of the heavens to be Mary and the son obviously to be Jesus. The twelve stars stood for the twelve tribes of Israel or the twelve apostles. The dragon, unable to harm the child, goes on to attack the woman's other children, namely us. This image of Mary echoes words in the Old Testament that describe a bride and are also applied to Mary: "Who is this that looks forth like the dawn, fair as the moon, bright as the sun, terrible as an army with banners?" (Song of Solomon 6:10).

In our creeds, we Catholics acknowledge that in heaven Jesus "is seated at the right hand of the Father." This expression means the place of honor and stands for Jesus' glory. Since Mary is the mother of Christ the King, we call her the Queen of Heaven. In Hebrew culture, the queen mother was often the power behind the throne. She wielded more authority than the king's wife. The queen mother's throne was often next to the king's, where she advised him and was able to intercede for petitioners.

When the apostles James and John asked Jesus if they might sit on his right and left in the kingdom, Jesus asked, "Are you able to drink the cup that I

quick quote...

As a believer who in faith thinks with God's thoughts and wills with God's will, Mary cannot fail to be a woman who loves.

—*Deus Caritas Est*
(God Is Love) No. 41

drink?" He was referring to the cup of suffering he accepted at the crucifixion. Mary deserves the place of honor in heaven because she drank that cup to the dregs.

Mary is also queen of the kingdom of heaven because she is the holiest human being that ever lived, other than Jesus himself. She is therefore called Queen of All Saints and Queen of the Angels. In art, Mary is often depicted wearing a crown, and at the end of the sixteenth century it became a practice to crown her image as a sign of devotion, something the pope still does today at certain shrines.

When Mary entered heaven, she entered into the glory that was hers as God's perfect creature. Mary showed more love for God than anyone else. We say that God crowned this lowly maiden the Queen of Heaven and Earth, Queen of the Universe. The idea of a heavenly coronation for Mary arose during the days of queens and empresses on earth. Mary's queenship is a position of honor more than a role of actually ruling. It means that Mary guards and guides us and deserves our love and veneration. In heaven, Mary prays for us, hoping for the day when we, her children on earth, will join her.

Mother of Mercy
Appearances on Earth

During recess, two small girls ran into school and breathlessly told their principal that they had seen the Blessed Virgin in the sky. The principal went outside and asked a teacher about it. The teacher said, yes, a cloud formation had resembled Mary. "What did you do when you saw Mary?" the principal asked the girls. One explained, "Well, first we said our First Communion prayers, and then we said the Pledge of Allegiance."

Every so often, people see Mary not just in clouds but in such unlikely things as oil stains and chocolate drippings. Some people claim to have visions in which Mary speaks to them. These visionaries can be mentally ill, or they can be saints. The first recorded Marian apparition was to St. Gregory the Wonderworker in the third century. In the vision of St. Catherine of Siena, when she was mystically wed to Christ, Mary was present. As a child, St. Thérèse of Lisieux was deathly sick when a statue of Mary in her bedroom seemed to smile at her, and she was restored to health. Nine-year-old St. John Bosco dreamed that Mary showed him a field of animals that transformed into gentle lambs, foretelling his work with youth. Later after he had opened his school for boys, he had another dream in which Mary revealed that his community would spread throughout the world.

If Mary is our mother, it follows that she will move heaven and earth to see that we are safe and happy. Her main goal is to draw us closer to Christ and his way of life. She knows that only this will bring lasting peace on earth and joy to our hearts. Apparently, sometimes Mary has even broken through the barrier that divides heaven from this world in order to advise and warn us.

I am all yours,
O Jesus, and all I have
is yours, through Mary,
your most holy
mother.

Medjugorje

Apparitions began in 1981 at Medjugorje in former Yugoslavia, now Bosnia-Herzegovina. Three of the six children who are the visionaries claim that Mary, as Queen of Peace, still speaks to them every day. Her five main messages, which are compared to the five stones in David's slingshot, are prayer, including the rosary; fasting; daily scripture reading; monthly confession; and frequent Communion. Millions of people have traveled to Medjugorje, where rosary chains turn gold and hearts turn to God. The Church, which moves slowly, is still investigating whether the apparitions are truly supernatural. For more information go to www.medjugorje.org.

During last two centuries, Mary has appeared to people more often than in all other centuries combined, leading some to think that the end of the world is near. Others point out that global communications have allowed apparitions to be more easily and quickly publicized than they were before. In the twentieth century, there were 386 apparitions reported. Mary has been seen in countries all over the globe. She usually appears to children, and sometimes they can see her when adults who are present can't. The Blessed Mother is always perceived as being extremely beautiful and radiating light brighter than the sun but harmless to the eyes. Mary's messages have been very similar: pray, do penance, and repent—turn away from sin and back to Christ her son.

Accepting Mary's apparitions as real is optional for Catholics. The Church never says that an apparition must be believed. On the contrary, the Church is quite skeptical and thoroughly investigates a supposed appearance before declaring the site "worthy of belief" or not. The local bishop is in charge of the process. One of the tests of a true apparition is looking for positive changes it effects in people's lives. The following main accounts are of the more popular and officially recognized appearances of Mary since the sixteenth century.

Our Lady of Guadalupe

In the most famous apparition of Mary in the Americas, Mary aligned herself with the lowly and marginalized. She reached out to and empowered the Aztec Indians of Mexico as Our Lady of Guadalupe.

Juan Diego and his wife Maria Lucia were converts who lived near Mexico City and walked the fourteen miles to the nearest church on Saturdays and Sundays. On December 9, 1531, Juan Diego, then a 57-year-old widower, was on his way to Mass before dawn. When he reached Tepeyac Hill, the former site of the pagan temple of the Aztec mother goddess Tonantzin, he heard what sounded like the music of strange birds and saw a rainbow encircling a cloud. A beautiful young Aztec woman appeared and beckoned to him. She was clothed in a rose dress, with a green and blue cape. Around her neck was a band with a black cross, and she wore the black sash that pregnant women wore. She addressed Juan as *Juanito Dieguito,* a term of affection and, speaking in his own language, asked where he was going.

The woman identified herself as the Virgin Mary, the mother of the true God. She said, "I wish and intensely desire that in this place my sanctuary be erected so that in it I may show and make known and give all my love, my compassion, my help, and my protection to the people. I am your merciful mother." She sent Juan Diego to the bishop with this request.

Since Juan Diego was only a lowly Indian, he was made to wait at the bishop's house, until he finally got to tell his story to Bishop Don Juan de Zumarraga, who did not believe it. Disappointed, Juan Diego left. But on the way back, the Lady appeared again. With tears Juan told her of his failure and humbly proposed that she send a better messenger. Mary explained that she had chosen him and promised that he would succeed.

The next day Juan Diego returned to the bishop. This time the bishop asked for proof that the Lady was the Mother of God. Returning home, Juan Diego encountered Mary again and asked for a sign. She promised one on the next day. But the next day Juan Diego's uncle was deathly ill, so Juan Diego stayed with him. On the following day the uncle asked for a priest from the monastery for the last sacraments. To avoid meeting the Lady, Juan Diego went a roundabout way to get the priest. However, Mary, undeterred at being stood up, came to him anyway. She asked, "What troubles you, my dear son? Where are you going?" When Juan Diego explained, Mary responded, "Let not your heart be disturbed, no matter what illness may be. Am I not here, I who am your Mother? Are you not under my protection? Your uncle is already well."

With that, Mary directed Juan Diego to climb to the top of Tepeyac Hill and pick roses. It was December, when nothing grew and the hill bore only cactus and thistles. Nevertheless Juan Diego discovered a variety of Castilian roses, which he gathered into his *tilma*, or cloak. When he brought them to Mary, she arranged them for him before he went off to see the bishop.

Standing before the bishop, Juan Diego told of his latest adventures. Then he loosened his *tilma* and let fall the many-colored roses. The bishop, with tears in his eyes, knelt before Juan Diego,

Our Lady of Hope

In 1871 in Pontmain, France, during the Franco-Prussian War, Mary appeared to six children in the sky over a barn. She wore a blue gown covered with golden stars, a black veil, and a golden crown. A red crucifix was in front of her and four candles around her. The townspeople were in fear as Prussian troops drew closer. Words on a white banner under her feet told the children to pray and foretold that the conflict would end. Ten days later, the war ended. All of the enlisted villagers, including the brother of the first two boys who saw Mary, returned home. In 1900 a basilica in honor of Our Lady of Hope was consecrated in Pontmain, France.

whose *tilma* was hanging from his neck. On the *tilma* was the portrait of his Lady, four feet, eight inches tall. The bishop took the miraculous *tilma* to the chapel. The next day Juan Diego returned home where his uncle, completely cured, explained that the Lady had come to him too and told him what to call her. No one knows today what this title meant, since Mary had spoken in the native dialect, but it sounded like "Guadalupe," a famous shrine in Spain, and so Mary became Our Lady of Guadalupe.

Two weeks later a new chapel stood on Tepeyac Hill, and the cloak was brought there. Nearby a hut was built for Juan Diego. During the next ten years, eight million Indians turned away from their pagan gods and were baptized, many through the appeal of Our Lady of Guadalupe and the witness of Juan Diego.

An enormous basilica was built at the bottom of the hill in 1709, and a new one was erected in Mexico City in 1976. Scientists continue to study the cloak of cactus fibers, which should have disintegrated in twenty years, yet after almost 500 years it

The flag of the Euro-
pean Union (EU), a
circle of twelve stars
on a blue back-
ground, was designed
by Arsene Heitz, who
was inspired by the
image on the Miracu-
lous Medal as well as
the woman with a
crown of twelve stars
in the Book of Revela-
tion. Heitz, who has a
deep love for Mary,
prays the rosary daily
with his wife. Coinci-
dentally the flag was
adopted on Decem-
ber 8, 1955, the feast
of the Immaculate
Conception. The de-
sign was acceptable
to non-Catholic coun-
tries with the under-
standing that twelve
is the symbol of full-
ness.

remains in good condition. In 1945, Pope Pius XII declared Our Lady of Guadalupe the patroness of the Americas, and in 1960, Pope John XXIII called her the Mother of the Americas. In Mexico in 2002, Pope John Paul II declared Juan Diego a saint.

The Miraculous Medal: The Immaculate Conception

Mary's appearance to a young sister in France marks the beginning of what is known as the Age of Mary. In 1815, when Catherine Labouré was an un-schooled nine-year-old in a French village, her mother died. A few months later a servant saw Catherine on a bureau in her parents' room, hug-ging a large statue of Mary and sobbing, "It is you, then, who are going to be my mother."

In 1830, against the wishes of her father, Cather-ine entered the Daughters of Charity on Rue de Bac, a community founded by St. Vincent de Paul. Six months later on a night in July, she was awakened by a boy in white about six years old standing at her bed and calling her. He said, "The Blessed Virgin awaits you."

Catherine followed the boy, who she thought was her guardian angel. He took her to chapel, which oddly was brightly lit. There Catherine heard the rustling of material and saw Our Lady come, bow to the tabernacle, and sit in the priest's chair. Catherine ran to her and knelt, setting her hands on Mary's knees. For at least two hours Mary ad-vised Catherine about her life and told her that God was going to entrust her with a mission. Then Mary predicted what the future of France and the world would be in forty years, and she wept. After the vi-sion, the boy led Catherine back to bed. As instruct-ed by Mary, Catherine told only her confessor, Fr. Aladel, about the vision, but he was skeptical.

One November evening while in chapel with the other novices, Catherine learned her mission. She saw the Blessed Virgin standing in glory to the right of the altar. Garbed in a white robe and a white veil that fell to her feet, Mary stood on a green snake atop a white sphere. In her hands was a golden ball surmounted by a cross, which Catherine took to mean the world that Mary was offering to God. Then the ball disappeared and Mary lifted her hands. They were covered with jewels of many colors. From some of them, rays fell on the white globe. Catherine interiorly heard a voice explain that the jewels were graces that Mary sent to those who asked for them. The gems that sent out no rays stood for unclaimed graces.

Then an oval frame appeared around Mary. Inside it were the words "O Mary, conceived without sin, pray for us who have recourse to you." Catherine was directed to have a medal cast with this design. Mary promised that whoever wore the medal and prayed the prayer would receive great graces and enjoy her special protection. When the frame revolved, Catherine saw an "M" surmounted by a cross standing on a bar. Under the M were the heart of Jesus with a crown of thorns and the heart of Mary pierced with a sword. Twelve stars encircled the picture. Catherine was also instructed to see that an altar with a statue of Our Lady of the Globe was built at the site of the vision.

Sister Catherine told Fr. Aladel and prayed, but nothing was done. Three more times Mary appeared. Finally Fr. Aladel mentioned the visions to the archbishop of Paris, who urged him to have the medals made. The "miraculous" medals were immediately popular. Millions of people wore them and told of wonders that occurred through Mary's intercession. In the meantime, Sister Catherine quietly cared for elderly men at a hospice, where she

a cool website...

To learn more about the Miraculous Medal and to receive a free one, you can visit www.amm.org. It is operated by the Vincentians at the National Shrine of the Miraculous Medal in Missouri.

was also in charge of the poultry yard. No one other than her confessor knew that Mary had appeared to this simple nun. The altar and statue were not completed until after her death in 1876. Catherine was declared a saint in 1947. Her remarkably preserved body rests in the chapel of her visions.

Our Lady of LaSalette

An unusual vision that conveys Mary's concern and sympathy for the world occurred early Saturday morning on September 19, 1846. Hired shepherd children Maximin Giraud, eleven, and Melanie Mathieu, fourteen, were watching eight cows and a goat in the foothills of the French Alps. After lunch in the warm sun, the two fell asleep. They awoke to find their livestock gone. After finding them, the two children saw down in a ravine a large globe of light reflecting colors. As they gazed in fear, the ball opened to reveal a woman weeping. She was seated with her face in her hands and elbows on her knees. The woman stood and crossed her hands on her breast.

The lady was of exquisite beauty and dressed like the peasant women of the region. She wore a long silver-white dress with small pearls of light. On her head was a glowing white headdress topped by high crown of varicolored roses that continually changed and shot forth light. The lady wore a shawl trimmed with roses, and she had a large yellow apron around her waist. On her feet were white slippers with gold buckles, which were surrounded by roses. From her neck hung two chains, one with a dazzling gold crucifix bearing a flesh-colored Christ. There was a hammer to one side and pincers to the other. These tools are interpreted as standing for reconciliation: the hammer (sin) pounded the nails in Jesus and the pincers (prayer and penance) removed them.

"Come near, my children," she invited in French. "Do not be afraid. I am here to tell you something of the greatest importance." Suddenly at peace, the children went into the ravine and crossed over a dried-up stream to the woman. The woman was still crying, her tears falling to her knees. She moved to the children so that her light enfolded them too. When she realized that they didn't know French, she changed to their language. She explained that because people no longer obeyed God's laws, her son was angry. They didn't observe the Sabbath and used God's name in vain, so her son's arm was heavy and crushing. She was holding it back and suffering for us. The woman went on to predict that as a result of sin, the crops would fail and a great famine would come.

Then the woman spoke to each child privately. After that she asked, "Do you pray well, my children?" When they confessed, "No," the lady responded that it was important to pray at night and in the morning, at least an Our Father or a Hail Mary. She observed that only a few old women went to Mass in the summer, while everyone worked on Sunday. She bemoaned, "During Lent they go to the meat shops like dogs."

In conclusion the woman said, "Well, my children, you will make this known to all my people. With that, she glided down the ravine and up the slope, her feet never touching the ground. The children followed. At the top of the slope the lady rose into the air and joy replaced her tears. The globe of light encircled her again, and she seemed to melt away.

Back in the village the children each told their story about the beautiful lady separately, and their stories matched. The village priest believed the children, but a local mayor bribed Melanie and threat-

fyi...

The United States bishops declared a shrine in Attleboro, Massachusetts the National Shrine of Our Lady of LaSalette in 2003. There every Christmas a Festival of Lights with more than 225,000 lights attracts a half million people. Visit www.lasalette shrine.org.

trivial tidbit...

Images of Mary have been observed to shed tears of oil, blood, or tears. Eyes of Marian pictures or statues have opened and closed. These phenomena are sometimes hoaxes and sometimes hallucinations, but sometimes they can't be explained.

ened Maximin, attempting to make them recant their story, all in vain. The villagers, including Maximin's father, heeded the Blessed Virgin's warnings. They began to practice the faith. A stream filled the dry bed and has never ceased flowing. Many cures were reported. A year after the apparition, 30,000 people processed to the site, where Masses were celebrated.

Maximin was taken to see St. John Vianney, the Curé of Ars, who didn't believe his story. Eight years later, St. John asked God for a sign if the apparition at LaSalette was authentic. He received it. A priest he had never met asked St. John what he thought of the appearances at LaSalette. That night the curé's table was covered with gold coins. In need of money for various good works, St. John picked up the coins. The next morning, the table was again covered with gold.

The bishop of LaSalette officially recognized the site in 1851, and the following year the LaSalette Fathers were founded, a community that carries out the ministry of reconciliation with a spirit of prayer and sacrifice. In 1879, on the spot where Mary appeared, the Basilica of Our Lady of LaSalette and a statue of her were completed. Unfortunately, both Maximin and Melanie went on to lead aimless, sometimes scandalous lives. And, no doubt. Mary, aware of the world and local news we hear about every day, still weeps.

Our Lady of Lourdes

The six million people who visit Lourdes, France, each year make it the most popular healing shrine in the world. It all began with a simple fourteen-year-old girl whose family was so poor that they lived in a room in an old prison. On February 11, 1858, Bernadette Soubirous, her sister, and a friend

Our Lady of the Golden Heart

Mary is believed to have come to Beauraing, Belgium, in 1932, appearing to five children: Albert, Gilberte and Fernande Voisin (ages 9, 13 and 15) and Andree and Gilberte Degeimbre (ages 14 and 9). Twice she appeared walking above a railroad bridge. Then thirty-one more times she came near a hawthorn tree by a Lourdes grotto at a convent schoolyard. She wore a white gown and veil. Sometimes she carried a rosary, and the children prayed at least part of it before or during the apparitions. Identifying herself as "the Immaculate Virgin" and "Mother of God, Queen of Heaven," Mary called for prayer for the conversion of sinners. During her last apparitions Mary showed the children her heart made of gold that sent forth rays of light. On the last day some adults in the crowd of 30,000 saw a flash of light around the hawthorn tree and heard a thunderclap. Since then, Beauraing has become a pilgrimage site where cures and conversions have occurred.

trivial tidbit...

Franz Werfel wrote the story of Lourdes in his book *The Song of Bernadette,* which was made into a popular movie of the same name.

were out collecting firewood. Weak from asthma and a bout with cholera, Bernadette fell behind. When she came to a stream, she heard a strong wind. In the rock grotto at the bottom of a mountain, she saw a bright light and in the midst of it was a young woman dressed in white with a blue sash. There were yellow roses at her feet and a rosary in her hand. As soon as the Lady smiled and made the Sign of the Cross with the rosary, fear left Bernadette. She knelt and prayed the rosary, with the Lady joining her in the Glory Be to the Father. The lovely Lady disappeared, but she would appear to Bernadette seventeen more times.

Word about the visions spread. Bernadette was questioned and sometimes threatened by lawyers,

Be creative in imitating Mary by bringing Christ to someone who is in need right now. It could be a family member, an acquaintance, or a complete stranger. You can do it with a personal visit, a note, a phone call, or an e-mail.

doctors, civil authorities, clergy, a teacher, and relatives. Crowds gathered whenever she went to meet the Lady, but only Bernadette could see and hear her. The Lady instructed Bernadette to do penance and pray for sinners. She also told her, "You will not have happiness in this life, but in the next." The Lady directed Bernadette to tell the priests that a chapel was to be built and processions held there. When Bernadette asked her identity, the Lady replied, "I am the Immaculate Conception." This convinced the priest that the apparition was real, because this dogma had only been declared four years earlier and Bernadette, who could barely read and write, was not familiar with the term.

On February 25, the Lady directed Bernadette to dig in the dirt and drink of the stream. Water appeared where she dug and continues to flow to this day. A few days later, a woman with two paralyzed fingers was cured when she put her hand into the water.

Bernadette became a Sister of Charity and died of tuberculosis at the age of thirty-five. She was canonized on December 8, 1933. Her body, remarkably preserved, lies in state in her convent.

At Lourdes today, a shrine is cut into the rock of Massabielle. There are four chapels to accommodate all the pilgrims. One chapel underground is the largest in Europe except for St. Peter's Basilica in Rome. The sick come to bathe in the waters of the stream and receive peace and comfort, if not physical healing. Today there have been more than 7,000 inexplicable cures at Lourdes. After a thorough investigation, the Church has declared 67 of them miraculous as of 2007. Each evening there is a candlelight procession during which pilgrims sing the hymn "Immaculate Mary."

Our Lady of Knock

The apparitions of Knock were never officially approved, but about a million people a year visit its site where the anointing of the sick takes place. Pope John Paul visited the shrine in 1979, giving it credibility.

On August 21, 1879, in the poor village of Knock in County Mayo, Ireland, about 7:30 at night, Mary McLoughlin, the parish housekeeper, went to visit a friend. At the south end of the church she saw a light silhouetting what looked like three figures. She thought they were new statues for the church. A half hour later, Mary was walking home with her friend's sixteen-year-old daughter, Mary Byrne. About 300 yards from the church they saw life-size figures of the Blessed Virgin, St. Joseph, and St. John about two feet off the ground. Mary stood in the middle, looking to heaven with her hands upraised. She wore a white cloak and had a large, golden crown with a rose over her forehead. St. Joseph, with gray hair and beard, was on the right and bent slightly to Mary. St. John was robed as a bishop. He held a book, and his right hand was raised in blessing. Behind the three was an altar with a cross on top and a lamb at its base. Small, brilliant lights covered the lamb and glittered around it.

Mary Byrne went to get her family, and soon they and neighbors came to view the scene. There were at least fifteen witnesses, ranging in age from six to seventy-five years. One boy approached so close to the figures that he could see the letters inside of the book. Though the rain continued, the figures remained dry. They never moved nor spoke. After two hours, the people left to pray with a dying neighbor. When they returned, the vision had disappeared.

Although some people thought the figures were

Elvis Presley recorded "Ave Maria" (certainly the most requested hymn for Catholic weddings and funerals).

Virgin of the Poor

Apparitions at Banneaux, Belgium, have also been approved by the Church. From January to March in 1933, the Blessed Mother is said to have appeared to eleven-year-old Mariette Beco eight times in a vegetable garden at the Beco family's cottage. The Virgin, enveloped in light and standing on a cloud, wore a white gown with a blue sash and a white, transparent veil. On her right foot was a golden rose. On her right arm she had a rosary with diamond-like beads and a gold chain and cross. Identifying herself as the "Virgin of the Poor," Mary promised to intercede for the poor, the sick, and the suffering. One day Mary led Mariette down the road to a spring. She also requested that a chapel be built at the site, and directed the child to pray much. When Mariette asked for a sign, Mary replied, "Believe in me. I believe in you." Miracles of healing have taken place at the spring, and today a small chapel stands at the site of the appearances.

a hoax, the parish priest recorded 300 miraculous healings that took place in 1880 at the church. Then in 1882, the Archbishop of Toronto, Canada, believed he was healed through Our Lady of Knock. Today a large basilica in Knock houses the remains of the old church. The small village was transformed into a place of pilgrimage.

Our Lady of Fatima

On May 13, 1917, Mary appeared in Fatima, Portugal, to three children: nine-year-old Lucia Santos and her younger cousins, Francisco and Jacinta Marto. The previous year an angel of peace had visited the children and taught them to pray. In 1917,

Pope John Paul II, a Marian Pope

Pope John Paul II, who had a deep devotion to Mary, dedicated his papacy to her. He took as his papal motto "Totus Tuus," a phrase directed to Mary that means "completely yours." He also included her monogram in a quadrant of his coat of arms. The third secret of Fatima predicted that a man in white would fall to the ground as though dead from gunshots. Pope John Paul was attacked on May 13, 1981, the anniversary of the first apparition of Fatima. Doctors declared that the bullet followed a strange zigzag path, avoiding vital organs. The Holy Father saw this as Mary's hand protecting him. The following year he went to Fatima and visited Lucy. He had the bullet that struck him placed in the crown of the Fatima statue. Pope John Paul again consecrated Russia to the Immaculate Heart of Mary in 1984, which he had declared a Marian year. Fittingly, this pope was a decisive figure in the surprising fall of Communist regimes, a seeming fulfillment of Mary's promise. In October 2000, the pope, along with 1500 bishops from around the world, entrusted the third millennium to Our Lady of Fatima.

the children were watching sheep when they saw a ball a light settle on a four-foot evergreen tree. Within the light stood a beautiful Lady dressed in white who said she was from heaven. She asked the children to meet her at the same time on the thirteenth of the month for the next six months. She asked if they were willing to suffer as reparation for sins and for the conversion of sinners. She told them to pray the rosary for world peace. Then she glided away into the sky.

Lucia's parents didn't believe her, and her mother scolded her. However, Mary appeared the next

The Worldwide Apostolate of Fatima, also called the Blue Army, is an organization founded in 1947 that has millions of members dedicated to spreading the word about Mary's messages. One of their programs is the International Pilgrim Virgin Statue, in which a statue of the Fatima Mary travels to dioceses and visits parishes. The Blue Army also arranges pilgrimage tours to Fatima and publishes the magazine *Soul*.

month as she promised and told the children to pray the rosary. She called herself Our Lady of the Rosary. Even when a government official threatened to boil the children in oil, they stuck to their story. Mary promised a miracle in October to prove they were telling the truth.

During one visit, rays shot forth from Mary's hands to earth, and the children had a vision of hell. Mary told them that sinners could be saved if they had devotion to the Immaculate Heart of Mary and made up for their sins. She instructed the children to add a prayer after each decade of the rosary. (See page 146 for a complete description of The Fatima Prayer.) The Lady also predicted a more terrible war if sin did not stop. She asked that Russia be consecrated to her Immaculate Heart, and that people receive Communion of reparation on the first Saturday of each month. She promised that Russia would eventually be converted and there would be peace if these things were done. Finally, the Lady gave the children a final secret that they were to tell no one. This secret, revealed in May 2000, foretold persecutions of the Church.

On October 13, the day of the promised miracle, 70,000 people gathered. Despite the rain, Lucy told them to close their umbrellas. Mary asked the children to have a chapel built on the site. She said that if the people prayed the rosary every day World War I would end. She said that sinners should stop sinning and ask forgiveness. When Mary vanished, the children saw scenes of the mysteries of the rosary in the sky. Simultaneously the crowd saw the sun turn white and begin to dance and shoot off colors that fell to earth. Suddenly the sun plunged to earth, and the people fell to their knees. When the sun stopped and returned to its place, they discovered that their clothes had dried.

As Mary had foretold, Francisco and Jacinta died

within a few years. The two were beatified in 2000. Lucy was to stay on earth in order to promote devotion to the Immaculate Heart. She entered the convent and lived until 2005.

Pope Pius XII consecrated Russia to Mary in 1952 and instituted the feast of the Immaculate Heart of Mary. Today there is a large shrine at Fatima where cures are reported every year.

TRUE DEVOTION TO MARY BEGAN WITH JESUS

Our Lady
Honoring Mary

or Catholics, Mary is a living reality. Devotion to her is a hallmark of Catholic life. We place her statue on our lawns and gardens, keep rosaries in our pockets, and walk in processions for the Feast of the Assumption. For almost two millennia, Christians have honored this woman by speaking and singing her praises; bestowing her name on people, places and things; writing poems and books about her; building cathedrals, composing music; and trying to capture her essence and express their love for her in various forms of art.

The Second Vatican Council and the *Catechism of the Catholic Church* encourage these practices. In his Apostolic Exhortation *Marialis Cultis* ("On Devotion to Mary"), Pope Paul VI urged us to develop new devotions suited to today's culture. Why? Because honor for Mary is always praise for Christ too. And the Catholic motto *"Ad Jesu per Mariam"* ("To Jesus through Mary") is still true. As Fr. William Joseph Chaminade observed, "We go to God through Mary, as faith tells us he came to us through her."

Imitation is the highest form of praise. Of all Marian devotions—past, present and to come—the best way to honor and show love for Mary is to strive to be like her. In imitating Mary, we are likewise imitating Jesus. This mother and son are both holy, that is, on fire with love for God and others. We can also imitate Mary's mission on earth of giving birth to Jesus. Cardinal Leo Josef Suenens pointed out that "true devotion to Our Lady makes us her instruments and co-workers in the invisible birth of Jesus Christ and the unfolding of his life in souls."

quick quote...

Have devotion to Mary, and you will see what miracles are.
—St. Don Bosco

Poetry and Legends

The tenth century saw the rise of Marian poetry. Some, like the Salve Regina, were beautiful lyric poems in praise of Mary. Other poems embellished stories about her life, particularly those in the apocryphal books. Gradually, new Marian legends were added, many borrowed from legends of the saints. One legend is about a priest ousted from his position who made a pact with the devil in order to get reinstated. When the priest repented, he was saved through Mary's intercession. In England in the twelfth century, miracle stories were compiled in collections such as *The Golden Legend* and the *South English Legendary*. Many of these legends featured Mary. She also had starring roles in the mystery-cycle plays. In addition, romances and secular poems often began or ended with an invocation to Mary.

The monk and preacher St. Bernard of Clairvaux (1090?–1153), who had an intensely personal devotion to Mary, glorified her as the advocate of sinful humanity in his poetry. St. Francis of Assisi (1181?–1226) wrote *Salutatio Beatae Virginis Mariae*, a greeting to Mary in which he hailed her as God's palace, tent, garment, handmaid and mother. Lines about Mary are also found in Dante Alighieri's *The Divine Comedy* of (1265–1321). In one beautiful prayer he has St. Bernard call Mary the "noonday torch of love" for those in heaven and "the living spring of hope" for mortals below.

History of Marian Devotion

In the first days of the Church, Christians focused on the risen Christ and his Second Coming. However, second-century saints like Justin Martyr, Ignatius of Antioch, and Irenaeus did mention Mary, comparing her favorably to Eve. Also, the fresco of Mary in the catacomb of Priscilla and the ancient prayer to her that begins, "We fly to thy patronage," hint of early Church devotion to her. (See the prayer *Sub Tuum Praesidum* on page 152.) Gradually, Christians began to view Mary as an important person in understanding Christ. It wasn't until the Council of Ephesus in 431 declared Mary to be the Mother of God, however, that devotion to her flourished and there was an outpouring of Marian hymns and prayers.

Again during the Middle Ages, beginning with the eleventh and twelfth centuries, there was another surge of devotion to Mary—shrines, cathedrals, pilgrimages, relics, penances and processions. People were drawn to flowery songs and religious fantasies like the apocryphal stories. This was the age of courtly love, when knights swore fealty to a lady, and troubadours sang in her honor. Monasteries developed a counterpart: Mary became Our Lady (Notre Dame) and more intimately Madonna (My Lady). Much of our language about Mary that today may be considered sentimental sprang from this feudal culture.

Great saints of this era, such as St. Francis and St. Dominic, honored Mary and encouraged others to do so. During this time, the divinity of Jesus was stressed much more than his humanity, and consequently people turned to Mary as someone more like them and therefore more approachable. Eventually, as with her son, Mary's holiness and uniqueness came to be emphasized and her humanness forgotten. Sometimes, overly zealous people even treated Mary as a goddess, giving her titles that rightly belong to the Holy Spirit, such as "Advocate" and "Comforter." In reaction to this idolatry, the Protestant reformers in the sixteenth century downplayed Mary's role. John Calvin insisted, *"Soli deo Gloria"* ("to God alone belongs glory"). Protestants banned and destroyed statues of Mary and the saints in the areas they controlled.

The Church dealt with the extremes in Marian devotion during the Counter-Reformation, which culminated at the Council of Trent. A new French school of spirituality and theology came into being under the guidance of Pierre de Bérulle and St. John Eudes. It focused on the importance of our being united with Christ and viewed Mary as a person who was perfectly identified with him. This led to renewed Marian devotion, but now the emphasis was on interior renewal.

Devotion to Mary reached another peak in the seventeenth century and was again often characterized by excess. The enlightenment of the eighteenth century, which scorned the "superstitions" of Catholicism, reined in the cult of Mary. So did the disbanding of the Jesuits in 1773. However, Marian apparitions in the next century and the proclamation of the Immaculate Conception in 1854 brought about the rebirth of interest in Mary. This flowed into the first half of the next century, culminating in the proclamation of the Assumption in 1950.

The Liturgy and Mary

In the liturgy, the Church gives praise and thanks for what God has done in Mary. All Marian celebrations are actually celebrations of Jesus. The Church first began to celebrate feasts of Mary in the fifth century. Today there is a book of forty-six Masses in honor of Mary that priests can opt to celebrate. Most are correlated with the liturgical year.

Days are established for honoring Mary under many titles, such as Our Lady of Pompeii on May 7

St. Mary Major and Our Lady of the Snows

After the Council of Ephesus, Pope Sixtus III erected the largest and oldest basilica in the West: the Basilica of St. Mary Major in Rome. It houses an icon of Mary reputed to be painted by St. Luke. The pope officiates at this basilica on certain occasions. On August 5, when we celebrate the dedication of St. Mary Major, during Mass Catholics drop white rose petals from its dome because of a legend. It's said that a church was first built on that site because Mary appeared to a wealthy couple in 352 and asked that a church be built where there would be snow. That night Pope Liberius dreamed the same thing. Although it was summer, the next day snow appeared on Esquiline Hill. As a result, a church was erected there and dedicated to Our Lady of the Snows. Today the National Shrine of Our Lady of the Snows in Belleville, Illinois, is one of the largest outdoor shrines in the country. See www.snows.org.

trivial tidbit...

Mary's birth is celebrated on September 8. This is why the Feast of the Immaculate Conception was set nine months earlier, on December 8. Similarly the Annunciation (March 25) is nine months before Christmas. Mary and John the Baptist are the only two saints whose births are celebrated. The feasts of other saints are celebrated on their day of death, their birth into heaven.

and Our Lady of Ransom on September 20. These days are usually observed in certain regions or in certain religious communities. Over and above these lesser commemorations, the universal Church celebrates the following Marian days with special Masses.

Feasts Honoring the Blessed Virgin Mary in the Roman Liturgy

❖ Solemnity of Mary, Mother of God—January 1
❖ Annunciation of Our Lord—March 25
❖ Visitation of Mary to Elizabeth—~~July~~ 31 May
❖ Assumption—August 15
❖ Birth of Mary—September 8
❖ Immaculate Conception—December 8

Obligatory Memorials

❖ Queenship of Mary—August 22
❖ Our Lady of Guadalupe—December 12
❖ Our Lady of Sorrows—September 15
❖ Our Lady of the Rosary—October 7
❖ Presentation of Mary—November 21

Optional Memorials

❖ Our Lady of Lourdes—February 11
❖ Our Lady of Mount Carmel—July 16
❖ Dedication of the Church of St. Mary Major—August 5
❖ Immaculate Heart of Mary—Saturday following the Second Sunday after Pentecost

Catholics continued to honor Mary to this day. Saints such as Louis de Montfort promoted prayers to Mary, including an act of consecration. Mary's apparitions in the nineteenth and twentieth centuries gave renewed impetus to people's focusing on her. At times, unfortunately, devotions took over their spiritual life, relegating the central components of our faith, such as the Eucharist, to the background. For example, instead of uniting themselves to the prayers and sacrifice at Mass, people prayed the rosary during Mass. Since in those days liturgy did not call for much participation, people turned to Marian devotions as an outlet for their spirituality.

The Second Vatican Council helped guide the Church back on the right track. When a separate document on Mary was proposed, the bishops voted it down, and she was included in the document on the Church. Later a proposal to give Mary the title "co-redemptrix" was rejected because it might be construed as implying that Mary was equal to Christ instead of subordinate. Mary was not to be viewed as standing next to Christ as through she had equal powers but as standing with us looking to Christ. At the same time, the bishops of the council set Mary before us as the Mother of the Church, who is to be honored and imitated. As a member of the Church, Mary shares in our call to holiness. She serves as a model for how to live out that call. Today, theologians continue to interpret Mary's life in contemporary terms so that she has meaning for us.

Scapulars

Wearing a Marian scapular is a sign of love for Mary and a commitment to live like her. Originally a scapular was the part of a religious habit that was placed over the head and hung down to the knees front and back. Today it usually refers to the sacramental that is two small pieces of cloth connected by strings and worn around the neck. A scapular is a sign of association with the spirituality of a particular religious order. A blessed scapular medal that has the Sacred Heart on one side and the Blessed Virgin on the other may be worn as a substitute.

Of the seventeen known scapulars, the most popular is that of Our Lady of Mount Carmel. In the past, children were enrolled with this scapular at the time of their First Communion. Enrollment, which must be done by a priest, lasts for life. The Carmelites were founded on Mount Carmel in Palestine in the twelfth century. There is a story that Our Lady appeared to St. Simon Stock in 1251 and promised that anyone who wore the Carmelite scapular until death—in other words, members of his community—would be assured of going to heaven. Centuries later, the small scapular became

Choose one new way
you will honor Mary
in your life. This can
be as simple as plac-
ing a statue of her in
your home or adding
a Hail Mary to your
night prayers.

Mary's Garden

Chaucer called Mary "the flower of flowers." This Old
Testament verse was applied to her: "I am a rose of
Sharon, a lily of the valleys" (Song of Solomon 2:1). In
medieval days, legends and love for Mary brought
forth Mary gardens, where different flowers related to
her were planted. More than 700 flowers and plants
have been named for Mary. Today, the Shrine of the
Immaculate Conception in Washington, D.C., and
some parishes grow a Mary garden with flowers
such as the following:

❖ Lily: Mary's purity. The gold stamens surrounded
  by the white petals stand for Jesus or for Mary's
  holiness.

❖ Rose: Its beauty, fragrance, and thorns signify
  Mary's role in salvation history. Mary is called the
  Mystical Rose. White roses stand for her joys; red
  for her sorrows, and yellow for her glories.

❖ Iris: Its deep-blue symbolizes Mary's fidelity, and
  its blade-shaped leaves denote her sorrows. The
  iris is the fleur-de-lis of France.

❖ Gladiolus: Its sword-shaped leaves symbolize
  Mary's sorrows. Gladiolus is Latin for "sword."

❖ Baby's Breath: Mary's innocence and purity as
  well as the breath of the Holy Spirit.

❖ Ivy (evergreen): Mary's faithfulness.

❖ Violets: Mary's humility and innocence. A legend
  has it that when Mary said, "Behold the handmaid
  of the Lord," violets blossomed outside her window and the Angel Gabriel blessed them as he
  left.

❖ Marigold (Mary's gold): Named for Mary, it symbolizes her simplicity and domesticity as well as

her sorrows because of its strong scent like burial ointments and because sometimes it "weeps" in the morning. A legend says that thieves who stole Mary's purse on the Flight into Egypt found it full of marigolds.

❖ Rosemary (Rose of Mary): Named for Mary. A legend is that it turned blue after Mary en route to Egypt spread the Baby Jesus' clothes out to dry on it.

❖ Thistle: A legend tells how the leaves of the plant became spotted when drops of milk fell on them while Mary was nursing Jesus.

❖ Blue Columbine: Our Lady's slipper, said to have sprung up where she walked.

Other flowers that are compared to things about or belonging to Mary include:

❖ Larkspur, Lily of the Valley: Mary's tears
❖ Forget-me-not: Mary's eyes
❖ Cornflower: Mary's crown
❖ Sweet Scabius: Mary's pincushion
❖ Peony: Mary's rose
❖ Morning Glory: Our Lady's mantle
❖ Bleeding Heart: Heart of Mary
❖ Periwinkle: The Virgin's flower
❖ Foxglove: Our Lady's gloves or thimble
❖ Parsley: Our Lady's lace
❖ Sage: Mary's shawl
❖ Daffodil: Mary's star
❖ Fuchia: Our Lady's ear-drops (earrings)
❖ Sweet Woodruf: Our Lady's bedstraw

You are the one who gave to human nature so much nobility that its Creator did not disdain His being made a simple creature!
—Dante Alighieri
The Divine Comedy

popular. Naturally anyone living a healthy spiritual life is not likely to commit a mortal sin. It is the prayers and good actions behind the sacramental that make a person more worthy of eternal life, not the wearing of the scapular alone.

Another scapular, popularly called "The Green Scapular," originated with visits of Mary to Sister Justine Bisqueyburu, a Daughter of Charity of St. Vincent de Paul in Paris, France. On her last visit to Sister Justine in 1839, the Blessed Mother appeared holding in her right hand her heart surrounded by flames and in her left hand a green cloth suspended from a green cord. On one side of the cloth was a picture of her as she appeared to Sister Justine. On the other side was Mary's heart with rays of light and pierced with a sword. Around the heart were the words "Immaculate Heart of Mary, pray for us, now and at the hour of our death."

The Miraculous Medal

The Miraculous Medal is called a "Marian microcosm," because its symbolism recalls the redemption as well as the love of the Sacred Heart of Jesus and of the Sorrowful Heart of Mary. The medal pinpoints the mediatory role of the Blessed Virgin Mary and the relationship between heaven and earth. See the complete story of the Miraculous Medal on pages 116-118.

May Altars

During the month of May, it is a tradition to create May altars for Mary, which are more correctly called "shrines." In homes and elsewhere, Catholics set an image of Mary in a place of honor and decorate this shrine with candles and flowers.

Two Saints Known for Devotion to Mary

St. Alphonsus Liguori (1696–1787) is a bishop, a Doctor of the Church, and the founder of the Congregation of the Most Holy Redeemer (the Redemptorists). Among his many writing is the book *The Glories of Mary*. A composite of information about Mary, it incited renewed devotion to her and has become a Catholic classic.

Born Louis Marie Grignion in France, St. Louis de Montfort (1673-1716) became a priest in France and wrote hymns to Mary and the books *True Devotion to Mary* and *The Secret of Mary*. He believed that just as God chose to initiate redemption dependent on her cooperation, so God continues the work through her.

Crowning of Mary

With the Council of Ephesus in 431, Mary began to be depicted wearing a crown. The ritual of crowning a statue or image of Mary became popular in the late sixteenth century. This devotion is often held during May, using a crown of flowers. In 1981, the Church issued a new rite for the crowning of an image of Mary. It includes a beautiful new litany with titles for Mary such as "Helper of the Redeemer," "Fountain of Beauty," "Untarnished Image of the Church," "Pride of the Human Race," and "Champion of God's People."

First Saturday Devotion

This devotion originated with the Fatima apparitions. At Fatima, Our Lady said to Lucy, "I shall come to ask...that on the First Saturday of every month Communions of reparation be made in atonement for the sins of the world." Later, when

St. Gertrude the Great (1256–1302) was a Benedictine nun who had mystical experiences that she recorded in a book. Once Jesus said to her, "I give you my own Mother as your protectress. I confide you to her care." Later, in an hour of trial, when a terrified Gertrude called upon Jesus, he replied, "I have given you my own most merciful Mother, and it is through her I will dispense my graces to you. Have recourse to her in all your necessities and you will surely find strength and consolation."

Lucy was learning to read and write in Spain, Our Lady reportedly appeared to her with a promise that she would assist at the hour of death with graces necessary for salvation all those who on the First Saturday of five successive months go to confession, receive Holy Communion, pray five decades of the rosary, and meditate for fifteen minutes on all the mysteries of the rosary.

Wedding Tradition

At the end of a Catholic wedding, the bride (and perhaps her mother or the groom) may go to Mary's statue and present a bouquet to her and say a prayer, entrusting her marriage to the Blessed Mother. This custom dates back to the seventeenth century.

Mary Candle

Mary is obviously a prominent person during the season of Advent. One Advent custom that unites us to her in her time of waiting is making a Mary Candle. A pillar candle that stands for Jesus is clothed with a mantle of white material tied with a blue ribbon. The cloth is removed on Christmas Day. The candle can be inscribed with the *chi-rho*, the symbol for Christ.

Months and Days for Mary

May is known as Mary's month. This is appropriate, for May is a month of newness, beauty, and the explosion of life. The month was named for the Roman goddess Maia. The Crowning of Mary often takes place on May 1. October is also a Marian month, the month of the rosary. Saturday is Mary's day every week. It is thought that this grew out of the belief that on the Saturday after Good Friday Mary alone had faith that her son would rise from the dead.

Marian Years

Periodically, the pope declares a Marian year to rekindle devotion to Mary. The last one was from Pentecost, 1987, to the Feast of the Assumption, 1988. Prior to that was the Marian year of 1954, a hundred years after Mary appeared at Fatima.

Images and Icons and Black Madonnas

The early Christians didn't produce art because of their roots in Judaism, which forbade the making of images. Later the Church came to understood that the reverence paid to religious paintings, mosaics, and statues is actually directed to the *subject* of the image. Furthermore, religious art was regarded as "the Bible for the poor."

Icon means "image." Religious icons are a highly symbolic form of art that originated in the Eastern Church and are regarded as a window into heaven. While painting an icon, the artist prays and fasts. Icons of Mary show her full-face, not in profile, to indicate that she keeps all viewers in sight. These Marian icons are of several different styles. One style shows Mary praying with her hands uplifted. Another, the tenderness style, shows her holding Jesus close to her, with her head inclined to him. In the style called "the one who points the way," Mary gestures to Jesus. One of the most loved icons is Our Lady of Vladimir, named for the city in Russia where it stayed for many years before being moved to Moscow. Many icons were destroyed in the eighth and ninth centuries, when religious pictures were regarded by

trivial tidbit...

About 700 congregations for women founded in the nineteenth and early twentieth centuries took a name with a title of Mary to show their devotion to her. Among these are the Sisters of Notre Dame, the Sisters of the Humility of Mary, and the Sisters of the Immaculate Heart of Mary. Congregations for men such as the Marists and the Marianists also were named in her honor.

Hernando Cortez, conqueror of Mexico, is said to have presented the Guadalupe shrine in Spain with a gold scorpion set with rubies, emerald, and pearls in gratitude for Mary saving him from a scorpion bite.

some (who became known as "iconoclasts") as a form of idolatry. The Crusades and the Protestant Reformation also led to the destruction of much religious art.

Black Madonnas are images of Mary that are dark for different reasons. Some are made of dark wood, some have been darkened by centuries of smoking candles, and some have been painted black. The Black Madonna statues usually show Mary seated with Jesus on her lap. There are more than 450 documented Black Madonnas. Most of them are from Europe's medieval period. The one considered the oldest, however, is Our Lady of Guadalupe in Spain, the namesake of the lady who appeared in Mexico to Juan Diego. See the complete story of Our Lady of Guadalupe on pages 113-116.

The Black Madonna of Czestochowa in Poland, supposedly painted by St. Luke, is one of the most famous. It depicts the Virgin Mary as "one who shows the way." Mary gestures to Jesus as our salvation, while Jesus, holding the book of Gospels in his left hand, blesses the viewer with his right hand. The painting arrived in the city from Jerusalem in 1382. In the seventeenth century, the monastery of Jasna Gora was saved from a Swedish invasion, which turned the tide of the war. In gratitude, the king of Poland crowned Our Lady of Czestochowa the Queen and Protector of Poland in the cathedral. The painting shows slash marks on Mary's face, left perhaps by swords during some attack.

Queen of Peace
The Rosary

On the cover of a recent *Time* magazine, there is an image of a rosary merging into a DNA model to accompany the cover story, "God vs. Science." Everyone recognizes that the rosary is a sign of faith. Undoubtedly it is the oldest, most popular, and best-loved Marian devotion. Joseph Haydn, eighteenth-century composer, always carried his rosary with him and prayed it. Chaucer, who lived in the fourteenth century, had his portrait painted holding a rosary. Martin Luther prayed the rosary all his life. The rosary was the favorite prayer of Pope John Paul II. Rosaries hang from rearview mirrors in cars and in Latin cultures are worn around the neck.

Catholics pray the rosary before or after Masses, during Eucharistic adoration, and at wakes. Popes and saints have prayed the rosary daily and have encouraged others to pray it. In her visits to earth, Mary has exhorted us to pray the rosary, especially for peace.

A blessed rosary is a *sacramental*, that is, an object whose use brings special graces through the prayers and merits of the Church. It is called "the Gospel on beads." Basic Catholic prayers we pray in the rosary are rooted in Scripture: the Apostles' Creed, the Our Father, and the Hail Mary. While praying these prayers, we also reflect on mysteries in the life of Christ. In this way, praying the rosary is like praying the memories of Mary. In fact, we are imitating her, who "kept all these things... in her heart" (Luke 2:19).

Moreover, the rosary is a very physical prayer. As we touch the beads, slipping them through our fingers, the rosary involve not only our bodies but also the stuff of creation—wood, metal, stone, plastic, even seeds, which are used to make some rosaries.

Origins of the Rosary

Although the Dominicans did much to promote praying the rosary, the story that it began when Mary gave a rosary to St. Dominic is only a legend. Christians were praying on beads a hundred years before him, and the original fifteen mysteries were only added two hundred years after him. The rosary has evolved through the centuries and continues to evolve. For example, five new mysteries were added recently, the first major change in the rosary in over 500 years.

How then did the rosary originate? Long ago when the Church prayed the 150 psalms, illiterate people substituted praying 150 Our Fathers (called *Paternosters* in Latin) on beads. (In Anglo-Saxon *bede* was the word for "prayer.") In the early eleventh century Lady Godiva (known for her legendary daring ride through the streets of Coventry, England) bequeathed her prayer-chain of precious stones to the church.

In the twelfth century, when the Hail Mary was formulated, people began praying this prayer instead of the Our Father on most of the beads. The rosary became known as Our Lady's Psalter. Sometimes genuflections and even prostrations accompanied each prayer.

Eventually, the rosary beads were grouped into decades (sets of ten) with another bead between each decade, and as each decade was prayed, one mystery was meditated upon. In time, there were three sets of five mysteries each: the Joyful, Sorrowful and Glorious. In 2002, Pope John Paul II added the fourth set: the Mysteries of Light, or Luminous Mysteries, which are events from Jesus' public life. These new mysteries filled the gap between the joyful mysteries of Jesus' early life and the sorrowful mysteries of his death.

How to Pray the Rosary

Some say that they can't pray the rosary because it requires doing two things at once: praying Hail Marys and thinking about a mystery, but this is no more impossible than it is to eat and watch television at the same time. The Hail Marys become a kind of background music while we reflect on the mystery. They are comparable to the Jesus Prayer or any mantra that is repeated as a springboard for union with God. Because of the soothing rhythm of the rosary's repetitions, some people pray it when they have trouble sleeping at night.

There are ways to insure that we are really *praying* and not just *saying* the rosary. Having a specific intention for the rosary helps motivate us to pray it well. Another tip is to spend a minute at the beginning of each decade concentrating on the mystery. At that time we might ask for the grace to grow in a virtue related to that event too. We can also be creative and pray our own mysteries, contemplating, for example, on five of Jesus' many parables, or on five of his miracles, or on the mysteries of our family or work lives.

Beginning

Make the Sign of the Cross with the crucifix and pray the Apostles' Creed.
On the single bead pray an Our Father.
On the three beads pray Hail Marys.
On the single bead pray a Glory Be to the Father.

For Each Decade

Pray an Our Father on the single bead. Pray ten Hail Marys. Conclude with a Glory Be to the Father.

Ending

Hail, Holy Queen, Mother of Mercy! Our life, our

Single-decade rings and bracelets are sometimes used to pray the rosary. Simpler yet, we can always pray the rosary on something readily available—our ten fingers!

In 1571, Turkish ships were poised to invade Christian Europe, Pope Pius V, a Dominican, called on all of Europe to pray the rosary, asking for the Blessed Mother's help. On the first of October the fleets met and fought. The Christians won, and the pope declared a new feast in honor of Our Lady of Victory. That became the feast of the Holy Rosary, celebrated on October 7. October is the month of the rosary.

Variations on the Rosary

❖ **The Living Rosary.** In a Living Rosary people representing the beads stand in a circle holding roses or vigil lights. One by one they lead the congregation in praying their assigned prayer and then place the rose or light before the image of Mary.

❖ **A Group Rosary.** Praying the rosary as a group is powerful. In some parishes, people pray the rosary before or after Mass. For those who are homebound or cannot find a group, there is a beautiful group recitation of the rosary on both CD and DVD available at www.actapublications.com.

❖ **The Family Rosary.** Father Patrick Peyton, CSC, was a dynamic promoter of the family rosary in the United States. He coined the motto, "The family that prays together stays together." In May of 2006, Pope Benedict XVI exhorted people to intensify the practice of praying the rosary in order to better understand the key moments of salvation history. He advised newlyweds "to make the praying of the rosary in the family a moment of spiritual growth under the maternal gaze of the Virgin Mary." A special booklet on how to pray the Family Rosary was written by Father Thomas Looney, CSC, and is available at www.actapublications.com.

❖ **The Fatima Rosary.** The Fatima Prayer originated from the Marian apparition at Fatima, Portugal, in 1917. It is commonly used, especially by the Blue Army of Our Lady of Fatima, as an additional prayer of the rosary, prayed at the end of each decade after the Glory Be to the Father: *"O my Jesus, forgive us our sins, save us from the fires of hell, lead all souls to heaven, especially those most in need of thy mercy. Amen."* While not part of the original rosary, many Catholics believe it to have been requested by the Blessed Virgin Mary during her apparition at Fatima.

❖ **Rosary Novenas to Our Lady.** A popular devotion written by Charles Lacey in 1924 and revised by Gregory Pierce in 2003 to include the Mysteries of Light is called *Rosary Novenas to Our Lady.* It calls for praying the rosary along with special prayers for twenty-seven days in petition and twenty-seven days in thanksgiving for a particular favor or help from the Blessed Mother. It is available at www.actapublications.com.

*sweetness, and our hope! To you do we cry, poor ban-
ished children of Eve; to you do we send up our sighs,
mourning and weeping in this valley of tears. Turn,
then, most gracious advocate, your eyes of mercy toward us; and after this our exile, show unto us the
blessed fruit of thy womb, Jesus. O clement, O loving,
O sweet Virgin Mary. Pray for us, O Holy Mother of
God, that we may be made worthy of the promises of
Christ.*

You many also finish the rosary by adding any or
all of the following prayers:

*O God, whose only-begotten Son, our Lord Jesus
Christ, has by his life, death, and resurrection purchased for us the rewards of eternal life, grant we beseech you that through meditating on these mysteries
of the most holy rosary of the Blessed Virgin Mary, we
may imitate what they contain and obtain what they
promise, through the same Christ, our Lord. Amen*

*May the divine assistance remain always with us.
Amen.*

*And may the souls of the faithful departed, through
the mercy of God, rest in peace. Amen.*

The Mysteries of the Rosary

Looking over the mysteries, it's easy to see why
Pope Paul VI called the rosary the epitome of the
Gospel. If you pray the entire rosary at one time or
over several days, the mysteries are prayed as follows: Joyful, Luminous, Sorrowful, Glorious. If you
pray the rosary everyday or most days, the traditional days for each set of mysteries are as follows:

❖ *Joyful Mysteries:* Monday and Saturday
❖ *Luminous Mysteries:* Thursday
❖ *Sorrowful Mysteries:* Tuesday and Friday
❖ *Glorious Mysteries:* Sunday and Wednesday

for your spiritual health...

Read *The Rosary
Prayer-by-Prayer:
How and Why We Pray
the Christ-Centered
Rosary of the Blessed
Mother* by Mary K.
Doyle with illustra-
tions by Joseph
Cannella. It is
available at www.
actapublications.com.

fyi...

In 1826, Pauline Jari-
cot, the founder of the
Society for the Propa-
gation of the Faith,
founded the Associa-
tion of the Living
Rosary. Fifteen people
were each assigned
one of the then fifteen
mysteries. They were
responsible for pray-
ing their one decade
every day for the rest
of their lives. The as-
sociation exists today,
with twenty people in
each group.

A university student sitting on a train next to an old man praying the rosary remarked, "I don't believe in such silly things. Take my advice. Throw the rosary out of this window and learn what science has to say." "Science? I don't understand," replied the man. "Maybe you can explain it to me." The student offered, "Give me your address and I'll send you some literature." Fumbling in his pocket, the old man drew out his business card. The boy looked at the card and burned with embarrassment. It read, "Louis Pasteur, Director of the Institute of Scientific Research, Paris."

The Joyful Mysteries

1. The Annunciation. The angel Gabriel was sent by God to Mary in Nazareth. He announced that God had chosen her to be the Mother of Jesus the Savior, the Mother of God. (Luke 1:26–28)

2. The Visitation. Mary went to help her older relative Elizabeth who was pregnant with John the Baptist. When Elizabeth heard Mary's greeting, she cried out, "Blessed are you among women, and blessed is the fruit of your womb." Mary responded with the Magnificat prayer. (Luke 1:39–45)

3. The Birth of Jesus. Mary gave birth to Jesus, wrapped him in swaddling clothes, and laid him in a manger. Angels appeared to shepherds and sang, "Glory to God in the highest heaven, and on earth peace among those whom he favors." (Luke 2:1–20)

4. The Presentation in the Temple. Mary and Joseph took the baby Jesus to the Temple to present him to God as the law required. There, Simeon and Anna recognized Jesus as the Savior. (Luke 2:22–38)

5. Finding of the Child Jesus in the Temple. After Passover, twelve-year-old Jesus remained in Jerusalem without his parents' knowledge. Three days later they found him in the Temple listening to teachers and asking them questions. (Luke 2:41–50)

The Luminous Mysteries

1. The Baptism in the Jordan River. Jesus had John the Baptist baptize him. John saw the heavens open and the Spirit of God descend on Jesus. A voice came from the heavens saying, "This is

my Son, the Beloved, with whom I am well pleased." (Matthew 3:17)

2. The Wedding at Cana. When wine ran out at a wedding, Mary appealed to Jesus and he worked his first miracle. He turned water into excellent wine. (John 2:1–12)

3. The Proclamation of the Kingdom of God. Jesus proclaimed the good news of God's love and salvation, saying, "The time is fulfilled, and the kingdom of God has come near; repent, and believe in the good news." (Mark 1:15)

4. The Transfiguration. Jesus took Peter, James and John up a mountain. While he prayed, his face changed and his clothing became dazzling white. He spoke with Moses and Elijah. (Luke 9:29)

5. The Institution of the Eucharist. On the night before he was crucified, Jesus shared a meal with his disciples and gave us the Eucharist. He offered himself for us under forms of bread and wine. In the Eucharist he is with us in a special way. (Mark 14:22–26)

The Sorrowful Mysteries

1. The Agony in the Garden. After the Last Supper, Jesus went to a garden with Peter, James and John. While he prayed, "My Father, if it is possible, let this cup pass from me; yet, not what I want but what you want," the apostles fell asleep. (Matthew 26:36–46)

2. The Scourging at the Pillar. Pontius Pilate, to satisfy the crowd, had Jesus scourged and handed him over to be crucified. (Mark 15:6–16)

3. The Crowning with Thorns. Soldiers stripped Jesus and threw a scarlet military cloak about him. They twisted thorns into a crown and placed it on his head and then put a reed in his

trivial tidbit...

The word *rosary* is linked to a legend. Supposedly a young monk in a vision saw his prayers fall from his lips as roses, which floated up to form a crown on Mary's head. In other words, praying the prayers is comparable to making a garland of roses for Mary. The rosary is sometimes called *chaplet*, which means "crown."

a cool website...

Learn how to make rosaries for the missions at www.olrm.org or www.rosaryarmy.com.

hand. Kneeling before him, they mocked, "Hail, King of the Jews!" (Matthew 27:27–31)

4. The Carrying of the Cross. Jesus, weak from being whipped and beaten, was unable to carry his cross to Golgotha alone. Simon, a Cyrenian, was forced to help him. (Mark 15:20–22)

5. The Crucifixion. At Golgotha (The Place of the Skull), Jesus was crucified between two criminals, yet he said, "Father, forgive them; for they do not know what they are doing." (Luke 23:33–46)

The Glorious Mysteries

1. The Resurrection. At Jesus' tomb an angel appeared to two women, saying "Do not be afraid; I know that you are looking for Jesus who was crucified. He is not here; for he has been raised, as he said." The angel sent the women to tell the disciples. (Matthew 28:1–10)

2. The Ascension of Our Lord. Jesus led his disciples to Bethany. He blessed them, then withdrew from them and was taken up to heaven. (Luke 24:50–53)

3. The Descent of the Holy Spirit. The Holy Spirit, promised by Jesus, came to the Church on Pentecost with signs of fire and wind. The apostles fearlessly went out and proclaimed the good news, and people of every language understood them. (Acts 2:1–13)

4. The Assumption of Our Lady into Heaven. Mary at the end of her earthly life was taken up body and soul into heavenly glory.

5. The Coronation of the Blessed Virgin Mary. The holy Mother of God, the new Eve and Mother of the Church, reigns in heaven, where she prays for and cares for the members of Christ.

Prayers to Mary

In speaking to Mary, Christians have praised her in beautiful words that have come down to us through the centuries. We fulfill her prophecy, "All generations shall call me blessed" (Luke 1:48). When we praise Mary, we are actually praising and giving glory to the God who made her what she is. Moreover, Jesus is certainly pleased to hear us compliment his mother, as any son would be.

Apart from set, formula prayers to Mary, there are our own personal conversations with her. We can approach her and talk with this warm and loving woman as easily as we speak with our best friends, knowing that she is really—though invisibly—present and concerned about us. At the end of the day, it's been a practice by many Catholics to pray three Hail Marys. But we can also simply hear Mary ask, "And how was your day?" and respond to her from our heart.

We can ask Mary for favors. She prays for and with us. *The Catechism of the Catholic Church* points out that, as the perfect pray-er, Mary is a figure (or archetype) of the Church. One of the earliest images of Mary shows her in the pose called *orans*, that is, with hands upraised with palms up, as we do when we pray the Our Father at Mass.

Mary takes our needs and concerns and presents them to God. This way our prayers are strengthened. Just as it helps to have people on earth pray with us, we benefit from the prayers of all of our friends in heaven, especially Mary. St. Louis de Montfort used a story to illustrate what Mary does to our prayers: A poor man had no money to pay the king rent. So he took what he had—a few bruised apples—to the queen, who was a friend of his. She polished the apples, set them on a gold dish, and gave them to the king, who was pleased with them.

The following are some favorite prayers to Mary.

151

In football, a "Hail Mary pass" is a desperate forward pass with only a very slim chance of success. It's usually a long pass at the end of a half when no other play can possibly work.

Hail Mary

This prayer is thought to have originated in the eleventh century as a salutation to Mary using the greetings of the Angel Gabriel (with the name Mary inserted) and of Elizabeth. The name "Jesus" was probably added in 1262. The ending petition was merged into the prayer later. The Hail Mary as we know it today became official in 1568.

Hail Mary, full of grace, the Lord is with thee; blessed are thou among women, and blessed is the fruit of thy womb, Jesus. Holy Mary, Mother of God, pray for us sinners, now and at the hour of our death. Amen.

Sub Tuum Praesidum

This prayer from about 250 A.D. is perhaps the oldest known prayer to Mary.

We fly to thy patronage, O holy Mother of God; Despise not our petitions in our necessities, but deliver us always from all dangers, O glorious and blessed Virgin. Amen.

The Angelus

The Angelus prayer in honor of the Incarnation—God becoming man—was made popular in the fourteenth century. We think the Angelus has its roots during the Crusades (1096–1270). The Crusades were military expeditions to regain the Holy Land from the Muslims. It is said that Pope Gregory IX ordered an evening bell to be rung to remind people to pray for the Crusades. Eventually, bells were tolled at 6:00 a.m., noon, and 6:00 p.m., reminding people to pray the Angelus. The Angelus is traditionally prayed at those times all year, except during Paschal time when the Regina Coeli is prayed instead.

The angel of the Lord declared unto Mary.
And she conceived of the Holy Spirit.
Hail Mary....

Behold the handmaid of the Lord.
Be it done unto me according to thy word.
Hail Mary....

And the Word was made flesh.
And dwelt among us.
Hail Mary....

Pray for us, O holy Mother of God.
That we may be made worthy of the promises of Christ.

Let us pray:
Pour forth, we beseech thee, O Lord, thy grace into our hearts, that we to whom the Incarnation of Christ, thy Son, was made known by the message of an angel, may by his passion and cross be brought to the glory of his resurrection. Through the same Christ, Our Lord. Amen.

The Magnificat (Canticle of Mary)

The Magnificat is Mary's hymn of praise found in Luke 1:46–55. Mary sang this canticle at the visitation after Elizabeth greeted her as the mother of her Lord.

My soul magnifies the Lord.
and my spirit rejoices in God my savior;
for he has looked with favor upon the lowliness of his servant.
Surely, from now on all generations will call me blessed;

fyi...

One touching French medieval legend with many variations tells of a young monk whose only talent was juggling. On the day before a feast of Mary, all the other monks prepared poems, flowers, artwork, and other gifts in her honor. That night a bright light drew them to chapel. There they saw the young monk before the statue of Mary juggling and dancing until he collapsed. The statue came to life, and Mary walked down and wiped the young monk's brow with her cloak.

for the Mighty One has done great things for me,
and holy is his name.
His mercy is for those who fear him from generation
to generation.
He has shown strength with his arm;
he has scattered the proud in the thoughts
of their hearts.
He has brought down the powerful from their thrones,
and lifted up the lowly;
he has filled the hungry with good things,
and sent the rich away empty.
He has helped his servant Israel,
in remembrance of his mercy,
according to the promise he made to our ancestors,
to Abraham and his descendants forever. Amen.

The Memorare

The great Benedictine monk St. Bernard of Clairvaux (1090–1153) is given credit for this well-loved
prayer. It was popularized in the fifteenth century
by a French priest named Claude Bernard. The word
Memorare is Latin for the prayer's first word, "Remember."

Remember, O most gracious Virgin Mary, that never
was it known, that anyone who fled to your protection,
implored your help or sought your intercession, was left
unaided. Inspired by this confidence, I fly unto you, O
Virgin of virgins, my Mother. To you do I come, before
you I stand, sinful and sorrowful. O Mother of the
Word incarnate, despise not my petitions, but in your
mercy hear and answer me. Amen.

Queen of Heaven (Regina Coeli)

This exuberant prayer, which dates back to the
twelfth century, is used in place of the Angelus during the Easter season.

O, queen of heaven, rejoice! Alleluia.
For he whom thou didst merit to bear, Alleluia.
Hath arisen as he said, Alleluia.
Pray for us to God, Alleluia.
Rejoice and be glad, O Virgin Mary. Alleluia.
For the Lord hath risen indeed. Alleluia.

Let us pray:
O God, who, through the resurrection of thy Son, our
Lord Jesus Christ, did vouchsafe to fill the world with
joy; grant, we beseech thee, that, through his Virgin
Mother, Mary, we may lay hold on the joys of everlast-
ing life. Through this same Christ, our Lord. Amen.

Hail, Holy Queen (Salve Regina)

A prayer from the eleventh or twelfth century, the
Salve Regina is attributed to various authors. The
Dominicans began singing it daily at the end of
Night Prayer about 1221. Now the Salve Regina is
one of the four prayers to Mary prayed in the Di-
vine Office. It is often chanted.
Hail, Holy Queen, Mother of Mercy,
our life, our sweetness and our hope.
To thee do we cry, poor banished children of Eve,
To thee do we send up our sighs,
mourning and weeping in this valley of tears.
Turn then, most gracious advocate,
thine eyes of mercy toward us,
And after this our exile,
show unto us the blessed fruit of thy womb, Jesus.
O clement, O loving, O sweet Virgin Mary!
Pray for us, O Holy Mother of God,
That we may be made worthy of the promises
    of Christ.

Prayer to Mary

This Marian prayer is one of four options to be prayed at the end of the Night Office. Possibly it was written by Hermann Contractus (the Lame), a severely deformed monk of the eleventh century, who composed beautiful music.

Loving Mother of the Redeemer,
Gate of Heaven, Star of the Sea,
assist your people who have fallen yet strive
*   to rise again.*
To the wonderment of nature you bore your Creator,
yet remained a virgin after as before.
You who received Gabriel's joyful greeting,
have pity on us poor sinners.
Amen.

Consecration to Mary

In this prayer, we offer ourselves to Mary and ask her protection and intercession so that we live out our baptismal promises. Technically "consecration" means setting something apart for God. This prayer is more like an "entrustment." In giving ourselves to Mary we are really dedicating ourselves to her son through her hands.

My Queen and my Mother, I give myself entirely to you; and to show my devotion to you I consecrate to you this day my eyes, my ears, my mouth, my heart, my whole being without reserve. Wherefore, good Mother, as I am your own, keep me, guard me, as your property and possession. Amen.

Hail, Star of the Sea (Ave, Maris Stella)

This prayer to Mary as star of the sea dates back at least to the ninth century.

Hail, bright star of ocean,

God's own Mother blest,
Ever sinless Virgin,
Gate of heavenly rest.

Taking that sweet Ave
Which from Gabriel came,
Peace confirm within us,
Changing Eve's name.

Break the captive's fetters,
Light on blindness pour,
All our ills expelling,
Every bliss implore.

Show thyself a Mother;
May the Word Divine,
Born for us thy Infant,
Hear our prayers through thine.

short prayer...

Our Lady, Queen of
Peace, pray for us!

Tota Pulchra

You are all fair, O Mary, and the original stain is not
in you. You are the glory of Jerusalem, you are the joy
of Israel, you are the honor of our people, you are the
advocate of sinners. O Mary, Virgin most prudent,
Mother most merciful, pray for us, intercede for us with
our Lord, Jesus Christ.

Mary, Help of Those in Need

Holy Mary,
help those in need,
give strength to the weak,
comfort the sorrowful,
pray for God's people,
assist the clergy,
intercede for religious.

As wax melts before fire, so do the devils lose their power against those souls who remember the name of Mary and devoutly invoke it.

—St. Bonaventure

May all who seek your help
experience your unfailing protection.
Amen.

Prayer of St. Ephrem the Syrian

Ephrem's writing was so elegant that he received the title "harp of the Holy Spirit." His teaching about Mary won him another title, "Marian Doctor." A doctor of the Church is a holy person who made great theological contributions to the Church. St. Ephrem died in 373.

Most Holy Lady, Mother of God,
you are the only one completely pure in soul and body,
and you surpass all purity, all virginity,
*   and all chastity.*

You are the sole dwelling place of all the grace
*   of the Spirit,*
and you far surpass the angels in purity
and in holiness of soul and body.

Turn your eyes toward me.
I am sinful and impure
and stained in soul as well as in body
with the passions and pleasures
that constitute the weeds of my life.

Set my spirit free from its passions.
Sanctify and restrain my thoughts
when they race toward adventurism.
Regulate and divert my senses.
Shake off the detestable and infamous tyranny
of my impure inclinations and passions.
Destroy in me the empire of sin.

Grant wisdom and counsel to my spirit
that is filled with darkness and wretchedness.

Help me to correct my faults and my failings.
Then, set free from the night of sin,
may I be worthy to glorify and exalt you
without reserve,
O sole true Mother of the true light,
Christ, our God.

Alone with him and through him
you are blessed and glorified
by every visible and invisible creature,
now and forever.

Litany of the Blessed Virgin Mary
(Litany of Loreto)

A litany is a traditional prayer of titles or qualities, after which a certain response is repeated. The Litany of the Blessed Virgin Mary was composed during the Middle Ages between 1150 and 1200. Its name comes from the shrine of the Holy House at Loreto where it was prayed. (See "fyi" on page 75.) The Litany of Loreto was set to music by Mozart.

Lord, have mercy.
Christ, have mercy.
Lord, have mercy.
Christ, hear us.
Christ, graciously hear us.
God, the Father of heaven,
have mercy on us.
God, the Son, Redeemer of the world,
have mercy on us.
God, the Holy Spirit,
have mercy on us.
Holy Trinity, One God,
have mercy on us.

fyi...

The Akathist Hymn is a Byzantine tradition song of praise of Mary and one of the oldest and most revered hymns. It may have been written by St. Romanos the Melodist, who died in 556, or it could have been composed in 636 to celebrate Constantinople's deliverance from the barbarians. This hymn, is always prayed standing, which is what "akathist" means. Reflecting the Marian beliefs of the primitive Church, the prayer addresses Mary by titles such as "Ladder to Heaven," "Pillar of Fire," and "Promised Land." The Akathist Hymn contains 24 strophes, one for each letter of the Greek alphabet.

(Response to all below: *Pray for us.*)

Holy Mary,
Holy Mother of God,
Holy Virgin of virgins,
Mother of Christ,
Mother of divine grace,
Mother most pure,
Mother most chaste,
Mother inviolate,
Mother undefiled,
Mother most amiable,
Mother most admirable,
Mother of good counsel,
Mother of our Creator,
Mother of our Savior,
Mother of the Church,
Virgin most prudent,
Virgin most venerable,
Virgin most renowned,
Virgin most powerful,
Virgin most merciful,
Virgin most faithful,
Mirror of justice,
Seat of wisdom,
Cause of our joy,
Spiritual vessel,
Vessel of honor,
Singular vessel of devotion,
Mystical rose,
Tower of David,
Tower of ivory,
House of gold,
Ark of the covenant,
Gate of heaven,
Morning star,
Health of the sick,
Refuge of sinners,

Comforter of the afflicted,
Help of Christians,
Queen of angels,
Queen of patriarchs,
Queen of prophets,
Queen of apostles,
Queen of martyrs,
Queen confessors,
Queen of virgins,
Queen of all saints,
Queen conceived without original sin,
Queen assumed into heaven,
Queen of the most holy rosary,
Queen of families,
Queen of peace.

Lamb of God, who take away the sins of the world,
Spare us, O Lord,
Lamb of God, who take away the sins of the world,
Graciously hear us, O Lord.
Lamb of God, who take away the sins of the world.
Have mercy on us.

V. Pray for us, O Holy Mother of God,
R. That we may be made worthy of the promises
of Christ.

Grant, we beg you, O Lord God, that we your servants
may enjoy lasting health of mind and body and by the
glorious intercession of the Blessed Mary, ever Virgin,
be delivered from present sorrow and enter into the joy
of eternal happiness. Through Christ, our Lord. Amen.

Prayer to Our Lady of Fatima

O Most Holy Virgin Mary, Queen of the Most Holy
Rosary, you were pleased to appear to the children of
Fatima and reveal a glorious message. We implore you,

fyi...

The Rosary: The Gospel on Beads for Grades 2-6 by Mary Kathleen Glavich, SND, is available from www.theobooks.org.

Jesus, show me
your mother;
Mary, show me
your son.

—attributed to St.
Ignatius Loyola

inspire in our hearts a fervent love for the recitation of
the rosary. By meditating on the mysteries of the redemption that are recalled therein may we obtain the
graces and virtues that we ask, through the merits of
Jesus Christ, our Lord and Redeemer.
Amen.

Prayer to Our Lady of Guadalupe

Dear Mother, we love you. We thank you for your
promise to help us in our need. We trust in your love
that dries our tears and comforts us. Teach us to find
our peace in your son, Jesus, and bless us every day of
our lives.

Help us to build a shrine in our hearts. Make it as
beautiful as the one built for you on the Mount of Tepeyac: a shrine full of trust, hope, and love of Jesus
growing stronger each day.

Mary, you have chosen to remain with us by giving
us your most wonderful and holy self-image on Juan
Diego's cloak. May we feel your loving presence as we
look upon your face. Like Juan, give us the courage to
bring your message of hope to everyone.

You are our Mother and our inspiration. Hear our
prayers and answer us. Amen.

Memorare to Our Lady of LaSalette

Remember, Our Lady of LaSalette,
true mother of sorrows,
the tears you shed for us on Calvary.

Remember also the care you have taken
to keep us faithful to Christ, your Son.

Having done so much for your children,
you will not now abandon us.

Comforted by this consoling thought,
we come to you pleading,
despite our infidelities and ingratitude.

Virgin of Reconciliation,
do not reject our prayers, but intercede for us,
obtain for us the grace to love Jesus above all else.

May we console you by living a holy life
and so come to share the eternal life
Christ gained by his cross.

Prayer to Our Lady of Lourdes

*Blessed, most pure Virgin, you chose to manifest your-
self shining with life, sweetness and beauty in the
Grotto of Lourdes. To the child, St. Bernadette, you revealed yourself, "I am the Immaculate Conception."
And now, Immaculate Virgin, Mother of Mercy, Healer
of the Sick, Comforter of the Afflicted, you know my
wants, my troubles, my sufferings. Look upon me with
mercy. By your appearance in the Grotto of Lourdes, it
became a privileged sanctuary from which you dispense your favors. Many have obtained the cure of
their infirmities, both spiritual and physical. I come,
therefore, with confidence in your maternal intercession. Obtain for me, O loving Mother, this special request. Our Lady of Lourdes, Mother of Christ, pray for
me. Obtain from your divine son my special request, if
it be God's will. Amen.*

Prayer to Our Lady of Mount Carmel

*O Most Beautiful Flower of Mount Carmel, Fruitful
Vine, Splendor of Heaven, Blessed Mother of the Son of
God, Immaculate Virgin, assist me in this my necessity. O Star of the Sea, help me and show me that you
are my Mother.*

fyi...

In the ark of the covenant, a wooden chest surmounted by two cherubim, God journeyed with the Israelites during the Exodus. Later this ark where God was present was placed in their Temple. It's easy to see why today Mary, the living temple of God, is referred to as Ark of the Covenant.

O Holy Mary, Mother of God, Queen of Heaven and Earth, I humbly beseech you from the bottom of my heart to succor me in this necessity. There are none that can withstand your power.

O show me that you are my Mother. O Mary, conceived without sin, pray for us who have recourse to thee. (repeat three times)

Sweet Mother, I place this cause in your hands. (repeat three times)

Amen.

Prayer to Our Lady of Sorrows

O Most Holy Virgin, Mother of our Lord, Jesus Christ: by the overwhelming grief you experienced when you witnessed the martyrdom, the crucifixion, and the death of your divine son, look upon me with eyes of compassion and awaken in my heart a tender commiseration for those sufferings as well as a sincere detestation of my sins, in order that being disengaged from all undue affections for the passing joys of this earth I may long for the eternal Jerusalem and that henceforth all my thoughts and all my actions may be directed toward this one most desirable object.

Honor, glory and love to our divine Lord Jesus and to the holy and immaculate Mother of God. Amen.

Prayer to Our Lady of Good Counsel

Most glorious Virgin, chosen by the eternal counsel to be the mother of the eternal Word made flesh, treasure of divine grace, and advocate of sinners, I, the most unworthy of your servants, beseech you to be my guide and counselor in the valley of tears. Obtain for me by the most precious blood of your son the pardon of my sins, the salvation of my soul, and the means necessary to obtain it. Grant that the holy Catholic Church may triumph over the enemies of the gospel and that the kingdom of Christ may be propagated on earth.

Prayer to Our Lady of Perpetual Help

Most holy Virgin Mary, who, to inspire me with boundless confidence, has been pleased to take that name, Mother of Perpetual Help, I beseech you to aid me at all times and in all places—in my temptations, in my difficulties, in all the miseries of life, and above all at the hour of my death—so that I may share in the resurrection of your son, our Lord, Jesus Christ.

Grant, most charitable mother, that I may remember you at all times and always have recourse to you, for I am sure that, if I am faithful in invoking you, you will promptly come to my aid. Obtain for me, therefore, the grace to pray to you unceasingly with filial confidence, and that, by virtue of this constant prayer, I may obtain your perpetual help and persevere in the practice of my faith.

Bless me, most tender mother, ever ready to aid me, and pray for me now and at the hour of my death. Mother of Perpetual Help, protect also all those whom I recommend to you: the Church, the Holy Father, our country, my family, my friends and enemies, and especially all those who suffer.

Prayer to Our Lady of Knock

This is an eleventh-century Irish litany of Mary.
Great Mary,
Greatest of Marys,
Greatest of Women,

trivial tidbit...

Edgar Allen Poe wrote a poem addressed to the Blessed Virgin Mary that was published in his book of poems.

quick quote...

Mary is the living womb in which, as in a second act of bodily motherhood, we are carried for the nine long months of our lives, until we at last come to the glory of redemption and resurrection.

—Edward Schillebeeckx, OP

quick quote...

In the plan of salvation, prayer to Mary is the ultimate recourse: with it we can never be lost.

—Charles Péguy

Mother of Eternal Glory,
Mother of the Golden Light,
Honor of the Sky,
Temple of the Divinity,
Fountain of the Gardens,
Serene as the Moon,
Bright as the Sun,
Garden Enclosed,
Temple of the Living God,
Light of Nazareth,
Beauty of the World,
Queen of Life,
Ladder of Heaven,
Mother of God,
Pray for us.

The Miraculous Medal Prayer

O Virgin Mother of God, Mary Immaculate, we dedicate and consecrate ourselves to you under the title of Our Lady of the Miraculous Medal. May this medal be for each one of us a sure sign of your affection for us and a constant reminder of our duties toward you. Ever while wearing it may we be blessed by your loving protection and preserved in the grace of your son. O Most Powerful Virgin, Mother of Our Savior, keep us close to you every moment of our lives. Obtain for us, your children, the grace of a happy death, so that in union with you we may enjoy the bliss of heaven forever. Amen.

Stabat Mater Dolorosa

This hymn from the thirteenth century is attributed to Pope Innocent III and to Jacopone de Todi, among others. Called one of the seven greatest Latin hymns, it is often sung at the Stations of the Cross and during Lent. It is also the Sequence for the Mass on the feast of Our Lady of Sorrows. This prayer recalls the anguish of Mary standing beneath the cross, the pain she bore as the Mother of the Redeemer. There is a parallel hymn about Mary's joy at Jesus' birth.

At the cross her station keeping,
stood the mournful Mother weeping,
close to Jesus to the last.

Through her heart, his sorrow sharing,
all his bitter anguish bearing,
now at length the sword has passed.

O how sad and sore distressed
was that Mother, highly blest,
of the sole-begotten One.

Christ above in torment hangs,
she beneath beholds the pangs
of her dying glorious son.

Is there one who would not weep,
whelmed in miseries so deep,
Christ's dear Mother to behold?

Can the human heart refrain
from partaking in her pain,
in that Mother's pain untold?

For the sins of his own nation,
she saw Jesus wracked with torment,
watching all his scourges rent.

She beheld her tender child,
saw him hang in desolation,
Till his spirit forth he sent.

O thou Mother, font of love,

touch my spirit from above,
make my heart with thine accord.

Make me feel as thou hast felt;
make my soul to glow and melt
with the love of Christ, my Lord.

Holy Mother, pierce me through,
in my heart each wound renew
of my Savior crucified.

Let me share with thee his pain,
who for all my sins was slain,
who for me in torments died.

Let me mingle tears with thee,
mourning him who mourned for me,
all the days that I may live.

By the cross with thee to stay,
there with thee to weep and pray,
is all I ask of thee to give.

Virgin of all virgins blest,
listen to my fond request:
let me share thy grief divine.

Let me, to my latest breath,
in my body bear the death
of that dying son of thine.

Wounded with his every wound,
steep my soul till it hath swooned,
in his very blood away.

Be to me, O Virgin, nigh,
lest in flames I burn and die,
in his awful judgment day.

trivial tidbit...

In the traditional Catholic prayer, the Morning Offering, we offer all the prayers, works, joys and sufferings of the day to God through Mary's hands.

169

trivial tidbit...

The emperor Charle-
magne wore a medal
of Mary around his
neck and asked to be
buried with a statue
of her upon his heart.

Christ, when thou shalt call me hence,
by thy Mother my defense,
by thy cross my victory.

When my body finally dies,
May the glory of paradise,
grant my soul eternity.

Amen.

To Mary, the Light of Hope

This is a novena prayer written by Pope John Paul
II and meant to be recited nine consecutive days.
Immaculate Heart of Mary,
help us to conquer the menace of evil,
which so easily takes root in the hearts of the people
of today,
and whose immeasurable effects
already weigh down upon our modern world
and seem to block the paths toward the future.

From famine and war, deliver us.
From nuclear war, from incalculable self-destruction,
from every kind of war, deliver us.
From sins against human life from its very beginning,
deliver us.
From hatred and from the demeaning of the dignity
of the children of God, deliver us.
From every kind of injustice in the life of society,
both national and international, deliver us.
From readiness to trample on the commandments of
God, deliver us.
From attempts to stifle in human hearts the very truth
of God, deliver us.
From the loss of awareness of good and evil, deliver us.
From sins against the Holy Spirit, deliver us.

Accept, O Mother of Christ,
this cry laden with the sufferings of all individual
human beings,
laden with the sufferings of whole societies.
Help us with the power of the Holy Spirit conquer
all sin:
individual sin and the "sin of the world,"
sin in all its manifestations.
Let there be revealed once more in the history
of the world
the infinite saving power of the redemption:
the power of merciful love.
May it put a stop to evil.
May it transform consciences.
May your Immaculate Heart reveal for all the light
of hope.
Amen.

Litany of Mary of Nazareth

The following litany is a modern one composed by Pax Christi, an organization that works for peace. For information, go to www.paxchristiusa.org.

Glory to you, God our Creator,
Breathe into us new life, new meaning.
Glory to you, God our Savior,
Lead us into the way of peace and justice.
Glory to you, healing Spirit,
Transform us to empower others.

(Response to all below: *Be our guide.*)

Mary, wellspring of peace,
Model of strength,
Model of gentleness,
Model of trust,
Model of courage,
Model of patience,

Of the four gospels,
the Gospel of Luke
presents the most de-
veloped portrait of
Mary. Also, this
Gospel's themes of
women, joy, the poor,
and the Holy Spirit
are all related to her.
An ancient tradition
holds that Luke was
an artist whose icons
of Mary with the child
Jesus are preserved:
one in Jerusalem, one
in Egypt, and one in
Rome. In the eigh-
teenth century, St.
Paul of the Cross,
after being denied ac-
cess to the pope,
prayed before this
icon in the basilica of
St. Mary Major in
Rome. He vowed to
promote the memory
of the passion of
Jesus and to gather
companions for this.
The result was the
Congregation of the
Passion of Jesus
Christ, popularly
known as the Pas-
sionists.

Model of risk,
Model of openness,
Model of perseverance,

(Response to all below: *Pray for us.*)

Mother of the liberator,
Mother of the homeless,
Mother of the dying,
Mother of the nonviolent,
Widowed mother,
Unwed mother,
Mother of a political prisoner,
Mother of the condemned,
Mother of the executed criminal,

(Response to all below: *Lead us to life.*)

Oppressed woman,
Liberator of the oppressed,
Marginalized woman,
Comforter of the afflicted,
Cause of our joy,
Sign of contradiction,
Breaker of bondage,
Political refugee,
Seeker of sanctuary,
First disciple,
Sharer in Christ's passion,
Seeker of God's will,
Witness to Christ's resurrection,

(Response to all below: *Empower us.*)

Woman of mercy,
Woman of faith,
Woman of contemplation,
Woman of vision,

Woman of wisdom and understanding,
Woman of grace and truth,
Woman, pregnant with hope,
Woman, centered in God,

Mary, Queen of Peace,
we entrust our lives to you.
Shelter us from war, hatred and oppression.

Teach us
to live in peace,
to educate ourselves for peace.
Inspire us to act justly,
to revere all God has made.
Root love firmly in our hearts
and in our world.
Amen.

A Mary-Themed Concert

On December, 17, 2006, in Shaker Heights, Ohio, the Church of St. Dominic Music Ministry, under the direction of James Carr, presented the Christmas concert "Mary—a Journey of Faith." Readings from the book *The Catholic Companion to Mary* wove together the musical numbers to form a beautiful, inspiring tapestry of Mary's life. The diverse pieces were sung by an adult choir, a children's choir, a trio, and individuals and were accompanied by a variety of instruments. During the Sufi song, *Hazrat Bibi Miriam*, six women performed a Mid-Eastern dance with large, brightly-colored scarves. Here is the program, including the location of suggested excerpts from this book, in hopes that others will produce an equally moving event. (Additional and alternate songs can be found on the Internet under "Marian hymns" and "songs of Mary" in any search engine, and different readings may be substituted from this book, the Bible, or other sources.)

Prelude: O Virgo Splendens   Anonymous 14th century

Read: page 9, paragraph 1
Hail Holy Queen (Sung by all)
Ave Maria   Jacob Arcaldelt

Read: page 10 paragraph 1, sentences 1–2; page 9, paragraph 2, sentences 1, 2
There Is No Rose of Such Virtue

Read: page 32, paragraphs 1, 2
A Dove Flew Down   Johannes Brahms

Read: page 32, paragraph 3; page 33, paragraph 1
Ave Maria   Franz Schubert
Ave Vera Virginitas   Josquin Des Prez

Read: page 39, paragraph 1; page 40, paragraph 2
Breath of Heaven   Amy Grant/Chris Eaton

Read: page 40, paragraph 4, sentences 1, 8–10; page 41, paragraphs, 1, 3
Magnificat   Jacques Berthier
Holy Is His Name   John Michael Talbot

Read: page 54, paragraph 1; page 55, paragraph 3
Remember Bethlehem   Jake Thackray

Read: page 56, paragraphs 1, 2
Angels We Have Heard on High (Sung by all)
The Virgin Mary Had a Baby Boy   John Leavitt
E la Don, Don   Anonymous Catalan
Joseph, Dearest Joseph   Arr. R. Vaughan Williams

Read: page 59, paragraph 2; page 60, paragraph 2; page 61, paragraph 1, sentences 3–5; paragraph 2
Maria Walks Amid the Thorn   Arr. Walter Ehret

Read: page 63, paragraphs 2, 3; page 65, paragraph 1
We Three Kings (Sung by all)   John Hopkins Jr.

Read: page 69, paragraph 4, sentences 1, 2; page 70, paragraph 2 (change opening phrase to "For about thirty years"); page 80, paragraphs 1, 2; page 81, paragraphs 3, 4
Lebedik   Klezmer

Read: page 27, paragraph 3
O Mary, Don't You Weep   Spiritual

Read: page 88, paragraph 1; page 92, paragraph 3; page 91, paragraph 1; page 94, paragraph 1
At the Cross Her Station Keeping   Anonymous 13th century

Read: page 94, paragraphs 2, 3; page 95, paragraph 1
Pietà   Tom Kendzia

Read: page 97, paragraph 1; page 99, paragraph 2
Joys Seven of Mary   English Traditional
Mary, Did You Know?   Mark Lowry/Buddy Greene

Read: page 10, paragraph 3; page 11, paragraph 1 (except last sentence)
Salamu Maria   African folk melody

Read: page 103, paragraph 2
Hazrat Bibi Mariam   Sufi devotional melody

Read: page 33, paragraph 2
Let It Be   Lennon/McCartney
Joy to the World (Sung by all)   George Fredrick Handel